THE BEST
SHORT GAME
INSTRUCTION
BOOK EVER!

HOME ENTERTAINMENT

Copyright 2009
Time Inc. Home Entertainment

Some of the material in this book was previously
published in *GOLF Magazine*, and is reprinted with
permission by Time Inc.

Published by Time Inc. Home Entertainment

Time Inc.
1271 Avenue of the Americas
New York, New York 10020

ISBN 10: 1-60320-088-6
ISBN 13: 978-1-60320-088-2
Library of Congress Control Number: 2009928253

Printed in China

We welcome your comments and suggestions about
Time Inc. Home Entertainment Books.
Please write to us at:
Time Inc. Home Entertainment Books
Attention: Book Editors
PO Box 11016
Des Moines, IA 50336-1016

If you would like to order any of our hardcover
Collector's Edition books, please call us at
1-800-327-6388. (Monday through Friday, 7:00 a.m.-
8:00 p.m.; Saturday, 7:00 a.m.- 6:00 p.m. Central Time).

Cover/book design: Paul Ewen
Cover photography: Angus Murray

GOLF
MAGAZINE

THE BEST
SHORT GAME
INSTRUCTION
BOOK EVER!

Guaranteed to save you strokes and get up and down every time

EDITED BY DAVID DENUNZIO

FROM THE
TOP 100
TEACHERS
IN AMERICA

GOLF
MAGAZINE
TOP
100
TEACHERS
IN AMERICA

Time Inc.
HOME ENTERTAINMENT

The Best Short Game Book—Ever!

The only short game instruction manual backed by 3,000 years of experience

BY the time you read this book your game will have undergone a serious transformation. Those strokes you've been wasting around the green by botching pitches and chips and leaving bunker shots in the sand? Gone. Forever. In their place you'll insert deftly crafted short shots that take advantage of your good drives and irons and save the ones that put you into trouble. Where your short game was once Clark Kent, it'll soar like Superman, swooping in at just the right time to correct the wrong and make the world a better place.

These are lofty claims, for sure, but they're made with confidence. This is not your ordinary instruction book. It's the third in a popular series that taps the collective wisdom of *GOLF Magazine's* Top 100 Teachers in America, the most trusted team of teaching experts in the nation. Together, these instructors bring over 3,000 years of experience to the lesson tee. They've seen it all. They know your strengths and weaknesses. More important, they have the tips, drills and techniques that allow you to repair your short game quickly and groove the moves you need to knock the ball close from around the green every time you set up with one of your wedges.

I applaud you for picking up this book. Obviously, you're aware of the shortcomings in your game, and recognize the importance of the short game to the numbers you pencil in on your scorecard. You're the minority—most golfers think the secrets to better golf are longer drives and stronger irons. While nobody will argue against the need to own a solid long game, you're going to lean heavily on your wedge play whether you can hit the ball 300 yards or barely squeak a drive to mid-iron range from the forward tees. The short game comes first, not only for scoring but also for building the swing fundamentals that make every club in your bag easier to hit.

If you're looking for ways to practice different elements of your short game, look for the "Drill" tags; techniques and new methods can be found under tags of the same name. And don't think for a second that these wedge, pitching, chipping and bunker-play lessons are only for the short-game challenged. Much of the instruction you'll read about in this book is the same the Top 100 Teachers give their more accomplished students, including a sizable number of PGA and LPGA touring professionals. Even at the highest levels of play, a solid short game—and the lessons that help shape and build it—never goes out of style.

DAVID DeNUNZIO
Instruction Editor, *GOLF Magazine*

Elite players like PGA Tour professional Hunter Mahan know what many amateurs don't: a solid shot game is the secret to going low.

CONTENTS

FROM THE
TOP 100
TEACHERS
IN AMERICA

HOME ENTERTAINMENT

Even when you miss the fairway or the green, landing short shots like this makes scoring easy.

1

YOUR SHORT SHOTS RULE!

What's the benefit of a good short game? It'll always be there when your full swing leaves you.

START HERE

The story is the same wherever you go: "I can't worry about my short game when my driving and iron play need so much work. I'll get to it when I'm happy with my long game." No wonder the average amateur handicap hasn't dropped in 50 years.

Yes, finding the fairway off the tee is critical to scoring, as is hitting the green with your irons and fairway woods. But no matter how skilled you are at either task, your scores hinge on the quality of your short game. A mid- to high-handicapper misses at least a dozen greens every round. That means you need to pull off a dozen good short shorts or you'll end up with a dozen bad bogeys. At least. That's just one of the reasons why you should start with your short game in your quest for lower scores. Top 100 Teacher Dr. Jim Suttie provides the rest on the following pages.

Why You Need a Solid Short Game

Improving your ability to hit solid wedge shots lifts the other areas of your game—and your enjoyment—to exciting new highs
—*Top 100 Teacher Dr. Jim Suttie*

The short game is often called "the game within the game," despite the fact it requires the same levels of feel, hand-eye coordination, mechanics, freedom of movement and creativity as your long game. It has earned this unique moniker because you can play most short shots a dozen different ways and still get the ball close to the hole (not always the case when you're on the tee box or hitting a mid-iron from the fairway), and do it with specialty and partial swings that generate specific amounts of carry and even more specific amounts of roll. Think about it this way: you rarely care what happens to your tee ball once it hits the turf (especially if it lands in the fairway), but you do when you're hitting a short shot into the green.

SOLVE THE PUZZLE

For most recreational players, the short game is a mystery, and sadly, something that's taken for granted, if for the only reason that it looks so easy. Show any new golfer a driver swing and a pitch swing and they'll tell you that the driver swing is the more daunting task. That may be true, but the penalty for missing a short-game shot is much more severe than missing a drive or an approach. You can always make up for an errant driver or a thinned iron with a good third shot from around the green. Miss that third shot, however, and the stroke is gone. Forever.

By the time you reach the end of this book you'll have learned all of the tools to solve the puzzle that is your short game. You'll be well on your way to lower scores. But there's more to becoming a savvy wedge player than swing mechanics and setup positions. You need to embrace your short game. You need to accept its importance. The following will make your journey much easier.

SHORT & SWEET

TOM WATSON
U.S. Open
Pebble Beach G.L.
June 20, 1982

In the last of a stirring series of head-to-head major championship duels, Tom Watson needed a par-par finish to tie Jack Nickalus, already in the clubhouse with the 72-hole lead. Watson's prospects looked grim after his tee shot on the 17th hole bounded into the rough behind the green. Undaunted, Watson smoothly slid his sand wedge under the ball and holed the chip for his only U.S. Open victory.

"Get it close? Hell, I'm going to make it!"
—*Tom Watson*

A GOOD SHORT GAME...
Helps you take advantage your long game

Most golfers think of the short game as a safety net—something to help you save par when you miss the green on your approach. But it's more than that—much more. On some holes, including almost every par 5, you're not going to sniff the green even after hitting two perfect shots. In these situations, your short game is more scoring opportunity than safety valve. It can get you into easy par range and, sometimes, easy birdie range. When you consider the frustration that comes from following two perfect full swings with a botched short shot, it's easy to see that your short game is there to help you capitalize on your full swing as much as it is to save it.

A GOOD SHORT GAME...
Demoralizes your opponents

Your playing partner bombs it off the tee—he's an easy 7-iron from the green, which he lands 20 feet from the hole. He two putts. Nice par.

You slice your drive. Badly. While you're hacking the ball back into the fairway, you catch glimpse of your opponent's smug grin. He thinks he's won the hole. You then stick a 60-yard half-pitching wedge to three feet and drain the putt. Funny, your man's grin immediately straightens.

There aren't any pictures on the scorecard to show how much better your opponent played the hole. Just two numbers: 4 for him and 4 for you. It's the same score, but you've won. You're in his head—he played the best he could and couldn't beat you. Short game to the rescue gain.

A GOOD SHORT GAME...
Gives you feel

All great scorers have great hands—by that I mean they "feel" distance with their eyes and then simply allow their natural hand-eye coordination to take over. That's a powerful existence. Yes, you need to follow some hard and fast rules when you hit short-game shots, but as you improve your skill from short range you'll come to rely more on instinct and feel, and this is the only way to eliminate tension from your swing. Some of the tips in this book will instruct you to visualize shot shape and trajectory before you pull the trigger. This is another aspect of feel, and once you get good at it with your short game you'll start using it when hitting your drivers and irons as well. It'll unlock a whole new world of shotmaking and fun. Better yet, you won't tense up when faced with a challenging drive or approach—your enhanced sense of feel and a tension-free swing will suddenly make every tough shot easy.

SHORT & SWEET

BOB TWAY
PGA Championship
Inverness Club
August 10, 1986

Bob Tway was in dire straits on the final hole of the year's final major. Tied with Greg Norman, who led in each of the previous three majors (winning one), Tway had landed his approach in a greenside bunker, while Norman had neatly placed his on the fringe. Ignoring the pressure, the slope in front of him and the lightning-quick green, Tway holed his blast for the win, setting off a series of last-minute, heartbreaking defeats that would come to partly define Norman's career.

"I was just trying to get it close."
—Bob Tway

A GOOD SHORT GAME...
Is the precursor to a good long game

In order to develop a good short game you must be free of tension and keep your swing as simple as possible—think of it as a miniature version of your full swing. The motions are the same—only the speeds and lengths are different, making these swings more art than science. Feel, imagination, and creativity are essential aspects of your short game, and when you build them into the swings you make around the green they'll transfer to the ones you make from the tee box and the fairway. There's an old story of a young Tom Watson approaching Byron Nelson for some swing help. Nelson obliged and eager Tom immediately pulled his driver from his bag. "No driver," quipped Byron, "not until you can show me you can hit a sand wedge."

A GOOD SHORT GAME...
Turns you into a "player"

Grooving a solid short game places you in a shot-shaper's mindset—you'll learn how to get creative with your swing. This is a good thing. The likes of Lee Trevino, Phil Mickelson, Seve Ballesteros, Chi Chi Rodriguez, Arnold Palmer, Jack Nicklaus and Tiger Woods are cut from this cloth. These are the players who know how to get the ball in the hole even when they leave their best swing at home. I'll never forget watching Seve Ballesteros hit 5-irons out of a practice greenside bunker at the 1989 PGA Championship at Kemper Lakes Golf Club. On each swing the ball came out high and soft, just like it would off a sand wedge. By the time you finish reading this book a greenside bunker shot to a tight pin will no longer scare you—nor will the thought of hitting this same shot with a 5-iron. While you may not remember the step-by-step protocol to hitting this shot, you'll fall back on the basics of trajectory and shot control to get it close.

A GOOD SHORT GAME...
Makes the game fun

Once you're able control your ball from short range you can play the game with anyone. You'll find that getting out of trouble around the green and making up for an errant shot is actually an enjoyable experience, not the fearful do-or-die situation it is for you right now. You may not believe me, but one day you'll look forward to the challenge of hitting a flop shot to a tight pin over a pot bunker—just another way to experience the thrill that is golf. Techniques like this unlock a whole new perspective of the game—the one that always makes you come back for more.

SHORT & SWEET

LARRY MIZE
*Masters Tournament
Augusta National G.C.
April 12, 1987*

To many it's the most miraculous shot ever to finish a major. On a day that saw nine players within a stroke of the lead with nine holes to go, and the highest winning Masters score in 15 years, local hero Larry Mize fought off two giants in a playoff to claim his only Masters. After watching Seve Ballesteros three-putt his way out of the tournament on the first playoff hole, Mize elliminated Greg Norman with his 140-foot roller-coaster chip on the second. The ball hopped twice, rolled halfway across the 11th green and dropped into the cup.

"I didn't think he'd get down in two.
I was right—he got down in one."
—*Greg Norman*

A successful short shot starts with outfitting your bag with the right collection of wedges.

2
WIN WITH YOUR WEDGES

A good short-game player always comes to the course with the right set of tools

PICK YOUR PAR-SAVER

There's nothing prettier than a well-built wedge. It shines. It's old school. It's equal amounts curve and right angles, carved—seemingly—from the hands of a seasoned craftsman who attended to it like it was the last one he would ever make. It's also high-tech, and engineered in such a way to make the gamut of short shots you face during the course of a round easier than ever to play.

If you've ever shopped for a wedge you know all this, and you're probably aware that the sheer number of designs, constructions, lofts, bounce angles and lengths make the wedge-selection process a fairly daunting one. But there's no way around it—you need, at the very least, the right combination of lofts to maximize your opportunities from short range. The information on the following pages is the advice you're been looking for. Choose well.

HOW TO

Build the Perfect Wedge Set

Learning the basics of wedge design and what differentiates one wedge from the next (other than loft) makes it easy to fill out your bag with the short-game tools that best match your game

THE GAP WEDGE

LOFT: 49-53 DEGREES

WHAT IT IS

Over the last few decades, clubmakers have done everything possible to maximize the distance potential of their iron sets. Lower and deeper CG locations, flexible faces, longer and lighter shafts, and of course stronger lofts, have made the current pitching wedge (48 degrees or even stronger) comparable to an old-school 8-iron. As a result, a relatively large "gap" has developed between most pitching wedges and sand wedges, which require 54 to 58 degrees of loft for obvious reasons. This development has created a strong need for a wedge that bridges the distance gap between these two clubs. Enter the gap wedge.

HOW IT WORKS

A gap wedge has many characteristics common to all wedges, including a wider sole (wider than a pitching wedge and other irons), more bounce, a bigger footprint (face depth) and heavier headweights. As a rule, a gap wedge fits comfortably between a pitching wedge and sand wedge in regard to loft, bounce and versatility. Because of these characteristics, a gap wedge can be useful for bump-and-run shots around the green, and even for longer bunker shots.

THE BOTTOM LINE

The key to finding the proper gap wedge for your needs is to first determine what degree of loft you need. Subtract the loft of your sand wedge from the loft of your pitching wedge and divide by two. That number is the loft that successflly bridges the gap between your two strongest wedges.

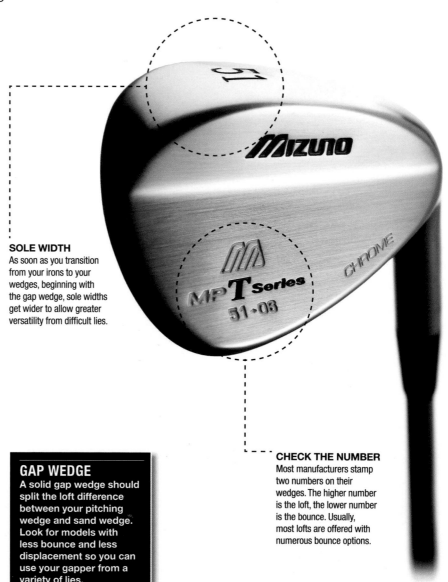

SOLE WIDTH
As soon as you transition from your irons to your wedges, beginning with the gap wedge, sole widths get wider to allow greater versatility from difficult lies.

GAP WEDGE
A solid gap wedge should split the loft difference between your pitching wedge and sand wedge. Look for models with less bounce and less displacement so you can use your gapper from a variety of lies.

CHECK THE NUMBER
Most manufacturers stamp two numbers on their wedges. The higher number is the loft, the lower number is the bounce. Usually, most lofts are offered with numerous bounce options.

THE SAND WEDGE

LOFT: 53-61 DEGREES

WHAT IT IS

Since the day Gene Sarazen was inspired by the sight of a duck landing on a pond, the design of the sand wedge has been unique, due largely to the specific job for which it's intended. Primarily, a sand wedge needs to resist digging in order to splash a layer of sand out of a bunker, carrying the ball into the air and onto the green.

HOW IT WORKS

To accomplish the task at hand, the sole of a sand wedge needs to be significantly wider than that of other irons, with ample bounce and less camber. Another important design element of a sand wedge is what some designers call "displacement," which is the distance between the leading edge and the ground. Obviously, because a sand wedge needs to resist digging, its displacement is typically the greatest of any club in your bag. If you've ever seen the famed Hogan Sure-Out, you probably remember it had a huge, wide sole and a ton of displacement. As a result, it was a great club for the average player who simply wanted to consistently get the ball out of the bunker without too much concern for shotmaking capabilities.

THE BOTTOM LINE

When it comes to choosing your primary sand club, it's critical that you consider the type of conditions you typically encounter on the course as well as your set makeup. However, as a general rule, for most recreational players it's best to err on the side of more sole width. This design characteristic provides greater effective bounce and simply makes the club easier to use in the sand. For reference, a typical low-bounce sand wedge has 8 to 10 degrees of bounce, while a medium-bounce wedge has approximately 12 to 14 degrees. High-bounce wedges can have as much as 16 degrees of bounce or more. Keep in mind that because a sand wedge typically has plenty of bounce and displacement, it's critical to keep your hands ahead of the clubhead when executing full shots from the fairway, or you'll catch the shot thin.

LOW CG
Most of the weight is in the sole. This low-cg design is a big reason why wedges are easier to hit than your other irons.

SAND WEDGE
If you carry four wedges, make your sand wedge as bunker-friendly as possible. Opt for lots of bounce (>10 degrees), extra displacement and extra face progression (leading edge ahead of the shaft centerline).

FACE PROGRESSION
On most wedges the leading edge sits in front of the shaft centerline, the exact opposite of an offset club.

A positive face progression makes it easier to slide the club under the ball on lob shots.

DISPLACEMENT
It's the distance between the leading edge and the ground. More displacement means the club will dig less.

LONG HOSEL
Wedges are bigger and heavier to accommodate high loft. Manufacturers counter the extra head weight with a longer hosel—a wedge design stalwart.

CAMBER
Think of it as the "roll" in the sole. Less camber is better for sand; more camber adds extra versatility.

THE LOB WEDGE

LOFT: 58-61 DEGREES

WHAT IT IS

The lob wedge is a high-lofted wedge that's made for use as a basic utility club. Short-game guru Dave Pelz built his first 60-degree wedge for Tom Kite in 1979; Kite added the club to his bag in 1980 and used it to win the Vardon Trophy in 1981. The mainstream "L Wedge" was designed by Karsten Solheim and became a standard in most sets of PING clubs.

HOW IT WORKS

The sole of the lob wedge is generally thinner than that of a sand wedge, and the bounce angle also tends to be smaller, making it more versatile in bad lies. More camber and less displacement also contribute to a lob wedge's versatility—they allow you to open the face at address without raising the height of the leading edge.

Another key characteristic is increased face depth (distance from leading edge to topline). As a rule, the more loft a wedge has, the greater face depth it requires to be playable (if you had a small face on a high-lofted wedge, there wouldn't be any room for a mis-hit). Lob wedges also tend to have slightly positive face progression (the measurement from shaft center line to leading edge). Positive progression means the leading edge is in front, or the opposite of offset. This element makes it easier to slide the club under the ball on lob shots, but also makes it easier to blade shots if your hands aren't forward of the clubhead through impact.

THE BOTTOM LINE

A lob wedge typically has 0-10 degrees of bounce, but can perform like a club with quite a bit more depending on sole width. For recreational players, more bounce is generally better than less. Keep in mind that a wider sole width increases effective bounce, while a thinner width decreases effective bounce. Make sure you're honest with yourself regarding your swing type and the playing conditions you typically encounter when selecting a lob wedge. Steeper swingers or those who play in softer conditions definitely need to avoid models

When you open the face of a typical lob wedge, the leading edge won't rise off the ground as much as it does when you open a sand wedge, making the lobber a bit more versatile.

LOB WEDGE
It's a good idea to select a lob wedge that performs well both in sand and on fairway and rough lies, so don't overdo the bounce angle and sole width (unless you want to make your lobber your primary sand club).

BOUNCE
Bounce is the angle of the sole, measured from the rear edge to front edge when the club is soled at address. The lob wedge at left has 4 degrees of bounce, while the bounce angle of the sand wedge at right measures 14 degrees.

More bounce makes it easier for a club to glide through sand, but it places a premium on contact from tight fairway lies.

SUPER LOB WEDGE

LOFT: 61-64 DEGREES

WHAT IT IS
In the early 2000s, Dave Pelz created a 64-degree X-wedge and offered it to Tour players after his research indicated that pros needed even more loft to stop the ball quickly on the green. Now, numerous Tour pros carry what some like to call a "super lob" for use in trouble situations.

HOW IT WORKS
Design characteristics of the super lob wedge include a very large face area (depth), low bounce, and increased face progression. A super lob functions in much the same way a lob wedge does, except with quite a bit less forgiveness due to the increased face progression and more loft. The super lob doesn't resist digging like a sand wedge.

THE BOTTOM LINE
Due to the extremely high-lofted nature of these clubs, they can be quite challenging to hit on full shots, particularly for less-accomplished players. But if used correctly, they can turn extremely difficult greenside shots into relatively easy ones. Not a lot of manufacturers offer super lobs, so if you're interested in adding one to your set you'll have to do a bit of research. Start with manufacturers that produce a wide range of wedge models—they're more apt to carry a specialty club like a super lob wedge.

Super lob wedges like the Titleist Vokey 62-degree model are gaining in popularity.

The extreme loft of a super lob wedge takes the pain out of tricky greenside pitches and chips. It works for elite players like Phil Mickelson because they know how to keep their hands ahead of the club at impact.

SUPER LOB WEDGE
If you play fast greens or have a difficult time getting the ball up on short pitches and chips, consider a super lob wedge. Only use it for full shots if you can consistently keep your hands ahead of the club at impact.

Get More Spin From Your Wedges

Three variables determine how much spin you can produce off your wedges. Choose the right combination to max out your backspin and hold every green.

—Top 100 Teacher Dave Pelz

THIS STORY IS FOR YOU IF...

1
You can't generate the spin needed to hold hard, fast greens.

2
You haven't given much thought to your wedge grooves and ball construction.

THE SITUATION

Every golfer needs backspin. Without a sufficient amount of it, stopping shots near the pin is very difficult (think about how many times your "good" short-iron or wedge shots have landed on the green and then proceeded to roll off the back). The bad news is that spin is becoming harder to get. Manufacturers keep lowering short-iron and wedge lofts (meaning they travel farther, but come in lower and harder) and the USGA has installed a new rule that will limit the spin capabilities of future wedge designs.

THE SOLUTION

The good news is that you're already making swings capable of producing shots with good backspin (at least occasionally). But your swing alone isn't enough. That cracks just one-third of the spin code. You also need the right ball and the right grooves. This dynamic generates anything from minimum to maximum spin, depending on how you fill out the following equation:

The Backspin Equation

$$\text{SWING QUALITY} + \text{GROOVE STRUCTURE} + \text{BALL TYPE} = \text{BACKSPIN}$$

SPIN FACTOR 1   **SPIN FACTOR 2**   **SPIN FACTOR 3**

FILLING OUT YOUR BACKSPIN EQUATION

Everyone has a Backspin Equation (you fill it out every time you hit a wedge, whether you realize it or not), and everyone's equation is different. This is why we each generate different levels of spin. Based on years of testing and research, we've discovered how to fill in the left side of the equation so the backspin number on the right is as high as possible. The trick is to address and improve all three of the spin factors, not just one or two.

SPIN DECISIONS
PGA Tour professionals like Justin Rose know that the secret to producing shot-stopping spin isn't only in the quality of your impact, but in the quality of your wedge grooves and the type of ball you put into play.

5 REASONS YOU NEED MORE SPIN

1. Faster greens
As greens get faster, the more spin you need to hold shots and make sure they don't run past the hole.

2. More forced carries
You used to be able to bump-and-run your way onto most greens. Not anymore. This places more emphasis on spin to stop high-trajectory approach shots.

3. Tighter pin positions
They're closer to the edges than ever before. You need spin as well as loft to get close to these ultra-tight pins.

4. Lower-lofted wedges and short irons
Manufacturers have been stealing loft from your scoring clubs right under your nose. With less loft you need more spin to hold shots.

5. New USGA ruling
Starting in 2010, new wedges won't be available with the grooves that have been proven to create the most spin.

SPIN FACTOR 1

SWING QUALITY

The swing that will give you the maximum possible backspin is one that provides solid and clean ball contact with an accelerating clubhead through impact.

FOR MORE SPIN
Make clean contact, catch the ball on grooves 3 through 6, and accelerate through impact

FOR LESS SPIN
Make grassy contact and decelerate

3 WAYS TO GET MORE SPIN FROM YOUR SWING

1. PLAY THE BALL BACK IN YOUR STANCE
This encourages you to strike the ball with a descending blow so you get less grass between the ball and the clubface.

2. SWING FROM SHORT TO LONG
You get proper clubhead acceleration when you take a shorter backswing and swing through to a full finish.

3. KEEP YOUR HANDS AHEAD OF THE CLUBHEAD AT IMPACT
This helps you strike the ball cleanly in the center of the clubface with minimal grass interference.

SOLID CONTACT
A solid "spinner" swing results in contact on the sweet spot (centered and covering grooves 3 through 6), so the clubhead doesn't wobble and lose control of the ball at impact.

DOWNWARD STRIKE
Because shots are usually hit from grass, you need a descending blow to trap a minimum amount of grass between the ball and clubface. Grass acts as a lubricant and diminishes spin-producing friction.

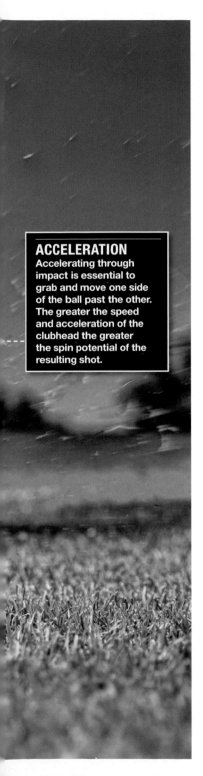

SPIN FACTOR 2

FACE GROOVES

Now that your wedge swing is capable of spinning shots, you need to examine the second part of your Backspin Equation. You need to make sure you play with wedges that have good enough grooves to provide the spin you desire.

A high-spin producing wedge must have enough loft and aggressive enough face grooves and friction to engage the ball's cover. Grooves that produce good backspin feature the qualities pictured here.

FOR MORE SPIN
Play wedges with box grooves
FOR LESS SPIN
Play wedges with v-grooves

3 FACE GROOVE FEATURES THAT ADD SPIN

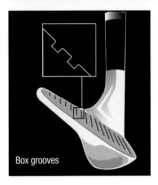
Box grooves

U-grooves
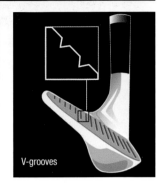
V-grooves

1. GROOVE SHAPE
In Pelz Golf Institute testing, box grooves were proven best for producing spin and stopping shots quickly [see chart, below], followed by U-grooves, V-grooves, and worn-out grooves of any shape. Of course, new grooves spin more than old grooves, and clean grooves spin more than dirty ones.

2. SHARP EDGES
The sharper the groove edges get (there are differences among today's models), the better they grab the ball's cover and produce spin.

3. LARGE VOLUME
The larger the volume of grooves, the more grass and water they can accommodate being smashed into them. This minimizes the amount of lubricant left to interfere with impact, making it cleaner (and the reason why most club companies only offer box grooves or U-grooves).

NOTE
The USGA has recently made a rule change that can affect your choice to use wedges with box grooves. If you're serious about getting more backspin, you must clearly understand how this new rule may or may not affect you [see the sidebar, next page].

HOW TO GET MORE SPIN FROM YOUR WEDGES

I recommend you get fit with a set of high-spin, box-grooved wedges. Combined with a quality wedge swing and a urethane-covered ball, you'll max out your Backspin Equation and get the shot-stopping power you need.

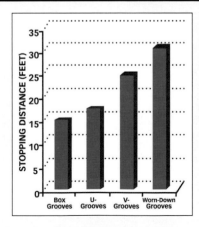

BOX GROOVES
93% less roll-out! compared to V-grooves

BOX GROOVES = MAX SPIN
Roll-out distance on 40-yard lob-wedge shots from light rough. Pelz Golf Institute.

SPIN FACTOR 3

GOLF BALL CONSTRUCTION

A glancing blow with enough friction to engage the cover of the ball is required to produce spin. But this presumes the ball is capable of being engaged by the clubface. If its cover is so slippery and hard that the clubface just slides past it with little or no engagement, then little or no spin will be produced. In order to generate the highest possible spin rate, you need to play a ball with a cover soft enough to be engaged by the grooves in the clubface. You have a choice between two covers: urethane and Surlyn. Urethane covers are unilaterally softer than Surlyn.

HOW TO GET MORE SPIN FROM YOUR BALL

The answer is easy: Play a ball with a urethane cover. Today's urethane models feature covers soft enough to produce high spin from typical wedge swings, and spin about twice as much as Surlyn (the choice for 70 percent of amateurs). True, urethane balls are more expensive, and Surlyn models are slightly longer off the tee, but check out the amount of spin you'll sacrifice with Surlyn [*chart, below*]. The only reason I see for so many amateurs playing Surlyn is their lack of knowledge on how much spin they lose (a factor of two!) by doing so.

URETHANE SPINS MORE THAN SURLYN

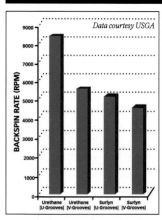

Data courtesy USGA

BACKSPIN RATE (RPM)

Urethane [U-Grooves] / Urethane [V-Grooves] / Surlyn [U-Grooves] / Surlyn [V-Grooves]

Spin rates for 8-iron shots with the ball in one-inch rough and half the ball above the grass surface.

There's a reason why PGA Tour players don't use Surlyn balls: Backspin and short-game control are more important to their scoring than distance off the tee.

FOR MORE SPIN
Play urethane-covered balls
FOR LESS SPIN
Play surlyn-covered balls

THE NEW GROOVE RULE AND YOU

The USGA has created a new rule to limit the backspin performance of grooves on lofted clubs. The rule downsizes groove volume and limits edge sharpness for all grooves manufactured after January 1, 2010 so they're equal to or less than the previously approved V-groove dimensions. PGA Tour players must use wedges conforming to the rule beginning on 1/1/10. The ruling will decrease backspin and increase the stopping distances pros typically achieve from grassy lies, and place more of a premium on hitting fairways.

How does the new rule affect you? If you're an amateur who wants more backspin, you realize the grooves you play are an important factor in determining the stopping distances you achieve on greens. In this regard, the USGA has been lenient. The rule gives amateurs (who don't play in Major/USGA events) a choice of which grooves to play until at least 2024. If you want to maximize your short-game backspin, you can legally play with box or U-groove wedges (manufactured prior to 1/1/10) until 2024. On the other hand, if you play with any wedge manufactured after 1/1/10 (like the pros will be doing), it must have grooves with spin performance at or below V-groove levels. This will limit you to mediocre spin performance. The USGA leaves this groove choice up to you.
—*Dave Pelz*

How to Choose the Correct Wedge

New research shows you can hit the ball up to 41 percent closer by making the right choice between your lob wedge and sand wedge

—*Top 100 Teacher Eric Alpenfels*

The old rule that the only wedge a good player needs is a sand wedge no longer applies.

The most common decision you're faced with as you move closer to the green is a simple one: Lob wedge or sand wedge? Thanks to my analysis of 540 short-game shots hit by golfers just like you, you can now know for certain that you've pulled the right club. This exclusive test, held at the Pinehurst Golf Academy with the help of Dr. Bob Christina, professor emeritus of the School of Health and Human Performance at UNC-Greensboro, is the first to provide a clear-cut guide to short-game club selection, and puts to rest the misconception that the only wedge a good player needs is a sand wedge. The test pitted 27 golfers against 10 familiar greenside lies. Each tester played every shot with both wedges, and only once, to simulate real-life playing conditions. The study unearthed significant differences in the performance of each club from different lies. What this means is that you can knock the ball closer to the hole simply by choosing the right wedge.

"This test is the first to provide a clear-cut guide to short-game club selection."

TURN THE PAGE TO SEE WHICH WEDGE CAME OUT ON TOP!

PITCH SHOTS

THE TEST

Study participants played 25- to 30-yard pitch shots from the fairway, rough and hardpan. The pitches were hit in random order and only once to simulate real-life playing conditions. In each case, the hole was cut in the center of the green—in other words, there was plenty of green available to land the ball.

THE OBSERVATION

Testers fared better with the sand wedge from hardpan, but hit the ball much closer to the hole from the rough and a normal fairway lie with the lob wedge.

WHY THE LOB WEDGE WON

Most of the testers felt the lob wedge allowed them to make a fuller swing, instead of an in-between one with the less-lofted sand wedge. That's a good thing—short-game spin and control come from accelerating through impact.

RESULTS: USE YOUR LOB WEDGE TO LAND PITCH SHOTS CLOSER

From the rough and the fairway, pitch shots hit by our testers with a lob wedge stopped an average of 11.5 feet closer to the hole.

TOP 100 TEACHER POLL

Q For what shot is the LW most useful?

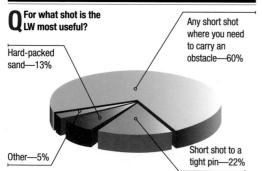

Hard-packed sand—13%

Any short shot where you need to carry an obstacle—60%

Other—5%

Short shot to a tight pin—22%

"Since a lob wedge has more loft and doesn't travel as far, you'll naturally be more aggressive and create the spin needed to land pitch shots close."
—Top 100 Teacher Anne Cain

PITCH FROM ROUGH

Distance to pin:	30 yds.
Distance to green:	23 yds.

Average distance remaining to hole:

Sand Wedge:	**28'10"**
Lob Wedge:	**17'2"** ☑

WINNER!

Lob Wedge 40% CLOSER!

TESTER COMMENT

"With the lob wedge I felt like I could take a full swing."

"Short-game spin and control come from accelerating through impact, regardless of the club you're swinging."

PITCH FROM HARDPAN

Distance to pin:	25 yds.
Distance to green:	20 yds.
Average distance remaining to hole:	
Sand Wedge:	**16'3"** ☑
Lob Wedge:	**24'6"**

WINNER!

Sand Wedge
34% CLOSER!

TESTER COMMENT

"The sand wedge allowed me plenty of room to let the ball run onto the green."

PITCH FROM FAIRWAY

Distance to pin:	30 yds.
Distance to green:	17 yds.
Average distance remaining to hole:	
Sand Wedge:	**27'9"**
Lob Wedge:	**16'6"** ☑

WINNER!

Lob Wedge
41% CLOSER!

TESTER COMMENT

"The lob wedge felt like I would lift the ball rather than scuff or blade it."

CHIP SHOTS

THE TEST
Testers played chips of 50 to 84 feet from (1) a clean lie to an easily accessible pin; (2) a clean lie with very little green between the fringe and the flagstick; (3) an uphill lie in the rough; and (4) a downhill lie in the rough over a bunker. Each shot was hit only once to simulate the pressure of having to hit a good shot on the first swing.

THE OBSERVATION
The sand wedge is the pick for chip shots unless you have to carry a bunker or other obstacle. In that case, the extra loft of the lob wedge makes it easier to clear the danger and stop the ball quickly.

WHY THE SAND WEDGE WON
According to our testers, a sand wedge is easier to control on delicate short shots. "It has to do with the bounce angle," says Top 100 Teacher Jerry Mowlds. "More bounce gives you more room for error in situations beyond sand shots."

TOP 100 TEACHER POLL

Q What is the primary advantage of a lob wedge over a sand wedge?

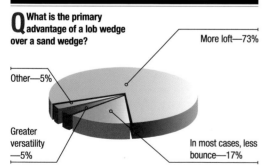

More loft—73%
Other—5%
Greater versatility—5%
In most cases, less bounce—17%

"Don't abandon your sand wedge just yet. Opening the face makes your sand wedge play just like a lob wedge, but with a touch of extra forgiveness due to the bounce." —Top 100 Teacher Jerry Mowlds

---

RESULTS: USE YOUR SAND WEDGE TO HIT CHIPS CLOSER

From the rough, from an upslope and to a tight pin, chip shots hit with a SW by our testers landed an average of 4 feet closer to the hole.

CHIP FROM UPHILL ROUGH

Distance to pin:	71 ft.
Distance to green:	32 ft.

Average distance remaining to hole:

Sand Wedge:	13'9" ☑
Lob Wedge:	19'4"

WINNER!

Sand Wedge 29% CLOSER!

TESTER COMMENT

"The sand wedge is heavier than a lob wedge, and feels easier to get through the grass to the ball."

DOWNHILL OVER AN OBSTACLE

Distance to pin:	84 ft.
Distance to green:	32 ft.

Average distance remaining to hole:

Sand Wedge:	32'4"
Lob Wedge:	24'1" ☑

WINNER!

Lob Wedge 29% CLOSER!

TESTER COMMENT

"With the lob wedge I just have more confidence that I can clear the bunker and keep the ball on the green."

"More bounce gives you more room for error in situations beyond sand shots."

CHIP FROM FAIRWAY

Distance to pin: 50 ft.
Distance to green: 29 ft.

Average distance remaining to hole:

Sand Wedge: **9'1"** ☑
Lob Wedge: **12'9"**

WINNER!
Sand Wedge 29% CLOSER!

TESTER COMMENT

"I just felt like I could control a sand wedge better because of the amount of spin."

CHIP TO A TIGHT PIN

Distance to pin: 38 ft.
Distance to green: 25 ft.

Average distance remaining to hole:

Sand Wedge: **4'11"** ☑
Lob Wedge: **8'6"**

WINNER!
Sand Wedge 42% CLOSER!

TESTER COMMENT

"On a shot that requires touch, I feel like I can take a shorter backswing with the sand wedge because it's heavier."

BUNKER SHOTS

THE TEST
Testers played bunker shots ranging from 43 to 52 feet to a center pin from the following situations: blast from a deep-faced bunker, standard bunker shot, blast from a buried lie.

THE OBSERVATION
Surprisingly, the lob wedge outperformed the club originally designed specifically to escape bunkers, although the two performed roughly equally from a buried lie.

WHY THE LOB WEDGE WON
The majority of testers felt the extra loft of a lob wedge made it easier to get the ball up and out of the bunker. "To do the same with a sand wedge, you have to open the face," adds Top 100 Teacher Dr. Gary Wiren. "But that raises the leading edge above the bottom of the ball and increases the chance of blading the shot. You're better off blasting with a lob wedge."

RESULTS: USE YOUR LOB WEDGE TO BLAST IT CLOSE FROM SAND

From non-buried bunker lies, blasts hit with a LW by our testers landed an average of 7.5 feet closer to the hole.

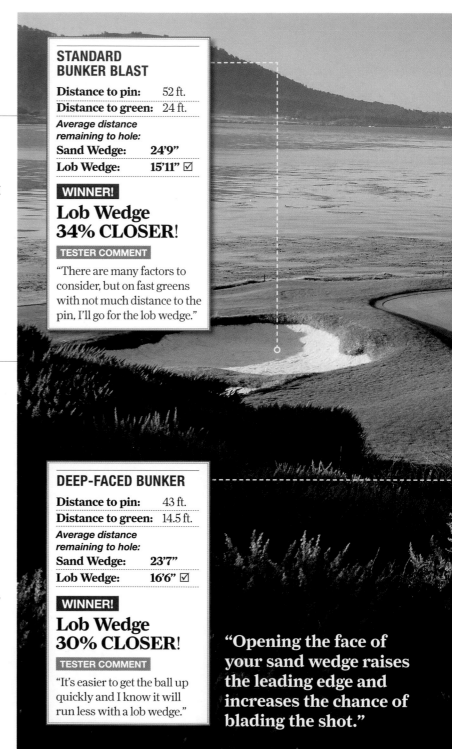

STANDARD BUNKER BLAST

Distance to pin:	52 ft.
Distance to green:	24 ft.
Average distance remaining to hole:	
Sand Wedge:	**24'9"**
Lob Wedge:	**15'11"** ☑

WINNER!

Lob Wedge 34% CLOSER!

TESTER COMMENT

"There are many factors to consider, but on fast greens with not much distance to the pin, I'll go for the lob wedge."

DEEP-FACED BUNKER

Distance to pin:	43 ft.
Distance to green:	14.5 ft.
Average distance remaining to hole:	
Sand Wedge:	**23'7"**
Lob Wedge:	**16'6"** ☑

WINNER!

Lob Wedge 30% CLOSER!

TESTER COMMENT

"It's easier to get the ball up quickly and I know it will run less with a lob wedge."

"Opening the face of your sand wedge raises the leading edge and increases the chance of blading the shot."

TOP 100 TEACHER POLL

Q Do you teach different swings for the LW and the SW?

No—98%

Yes—2%

"When you're swinging your lob wedge you're dealing with more loft, so the tendency is to come up short. Stay aggressive, just like you do with any of your wedges."—Top 100 Brady Riggs

BURIED-LIE BUNKER SHOT

Distance to pin:	52 ft.
Distance to green:	24 ft.

Average distance remaining to hole:

Sand Wedge:	**31'1"**	☑
Lob Wedge:	**30'9"**	☑

WINNER!

Toss-Up!

TESTER COMMENT

"I'll use either one in this situation, it just depends upon the distance to the pin."

Lower scores can be yours by eliminating the weak spots in your game. The trick: you've got to find them first.

3

SHORT GAME SKILLS TEST

Discovering your weaknesses is the first step toward eliminating them for good

GET IN TOUCH WITH YOUR WEDGE PLAY

There's nothing worse—or more frustrating—than knowing that a part of your game needs work (like you do with your short shots, as evidenced by your purchase of this book), but not knowing how to go about the business of making repairs. Relax. All of the techniques, tips, swing thoughts and drills you need to overhaul your game are in Chapters 4-8. What you'll find in this chapter is a systematic way to narrow your "to-do" list so you can concentrate on the areas of your short game that consistently cause you to lose strokes, and not waste time practicing moves you already have down pat. You're going to be tested on your ability to hit a variety of wedge, chip, pitch and bunker shots. Don't worry—there are no wrong answers, just a heavy dose of invaluable insight into the golfer your are and the one you want to be.

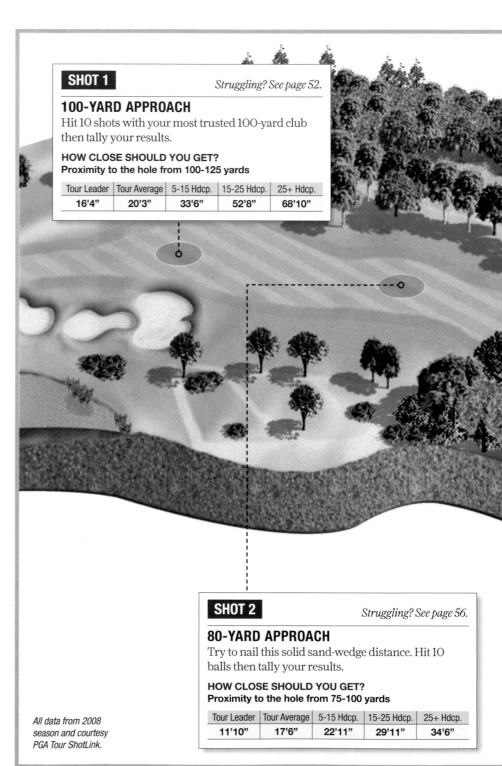

Struggling? See page 52.

SHOT 1

100-YARD APPROACH

Hit 10 shots with your most trusted 100-yard club then tally your results.

HOW CLOSE SHOULD YOU GET?
Proximity to the hole from 100-125 yards

Tour Leader	Tour Average	5-15 Hdcp.	15-25 Hdcp.	25+ Hdcp.
16'4"	20'3"	33'6"	52'8"	68'10"

Struggling? See page 56.

SHOT 2

80-YARD APPROACH

Try to nail this solid sand-wedge distance. Hit 10 balls then tally your results.

HOW CLOSE SHOULD YOU GET?
Proximity to the hole from 75-100 yards

Tour Leader	Tour Average	5-15 Hdcp.	15-25 Hdcp.	25+ Hdcp.
11'10"	17'6"	22'11"	29'11"	34'6"

All data from 2008 season and courtesy PGA Tour ShotLink.

HOW TO

Find Your Weak Spots

Take our scoring-zone skills test to discover where you're losing the most strokes and the weak spots in your short game that require immediate attention and repair.

—The Editors

RATE YOUR WEDGE SHOTS

Head out to the course and find a nice flat hole with a gently sloped green. (Or just build this hole in your mind at the range). Hit 10 balls from each of the stations pictured at right, scoring them using the Shot Rating Guide on the opposite page. Use the table below to tally your results and see where your wedge game is in need of the most help. Perform this test (and the remaining tests in this chapter) later in the season to find out how you're progressing (or falling back).

ADD IT UP
Tally the results of each test using the scorecard at right

	100 YARDS	80 YARDS	60 YARDS	40 YARDS
#1				
#2				
#3				
#4				
#5				
#6				
#7				
#8				
#9				
#10				
TOTAL				

RATING SCALE: ACE > 15   **SOLID** 10-14   **FAIR** 5-10   **OUCH** < 5

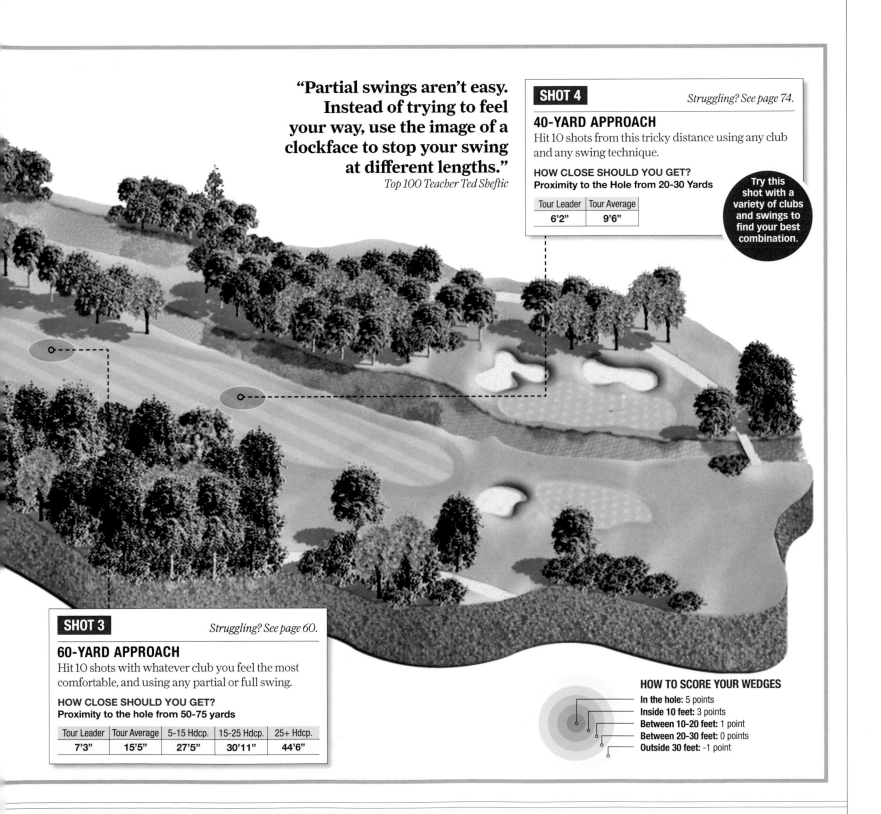

> **"Partial swings aren't easy. Instead of trying to feel your way, use the image of a clockface to stop your swing at different lengths."**
>
> *Top 100 Teacher Ted Sheftic*

SHOT 4

Struggling? See page 74.

40-YARD APPROACH

Hit 10 shots from this tricky distance using any club and any swing technique.

HOW CLOSE SHOULD YOU GET?
Proximity to the Hole from 20-30 Yards

Tour Leader	Tour Average
6'2"	9'6"

Try this shot with a variety of clubs and swings to find your best combination.

SHOT 3

Struggling? See page 60.

60-YARD APPROACH

Hit 10 shots with whatever club you feel the most comfortable, and using any partial or full swing.

HOW CLOSE SHOULD YOU GET?
Proximity to the hole from 50-75 yards

Tour Leader	Tour Average	5-15 Hdcp.	15-25 Hdcp.	25+ Hdcp.
7'3"	15'5"	27'5"	30'11"	44'6"

HOW TO SCORE YOUR WEDGES

In the hole: 5 points
Inside 10 feet: 3 points
Between 10-20 feet: 1 point
Between 20-30 feet: 0 points
Outside 30 feet: -1 point

Rate Your Pitch Shots

TAKE THE TEST!

Head out to the course and find a hole with a nice flat green. Walk to a point approximately 15 yards from the edge of the green, then look for a clean spot in the fairway. Mark a second spot roughtly the same distance from the hole but in the rough. (Again, build this hole in your mind if you're performing this test at the range.) Hit 10 balls from each of the stations pictured at right, first to a middle pin position, then to a front pin positions. Rate your pitches using the Shot Rating Guide on the opposite page and tally your results in the table below. The results should give you a good idea on the amount of work you should dedicate to your pitching game in the coming months.

ADD IT UP
Tally the results of each test using the scorecard at right.

	STANDARD PITCH	PITCH TO A TIGHT PIN	PITCH FROM ROUGH	PITCH FROM ROUGH TO A TIGHT PIN
#1				
#2				
#3				
#4				
#5				
#6				
#7				
#8				
#9				
#10				
TOTAL				

RATING SCALE: ACE > 20 **SOLID** 15-20 **FAIR** 10-15 **OUCH** < 10

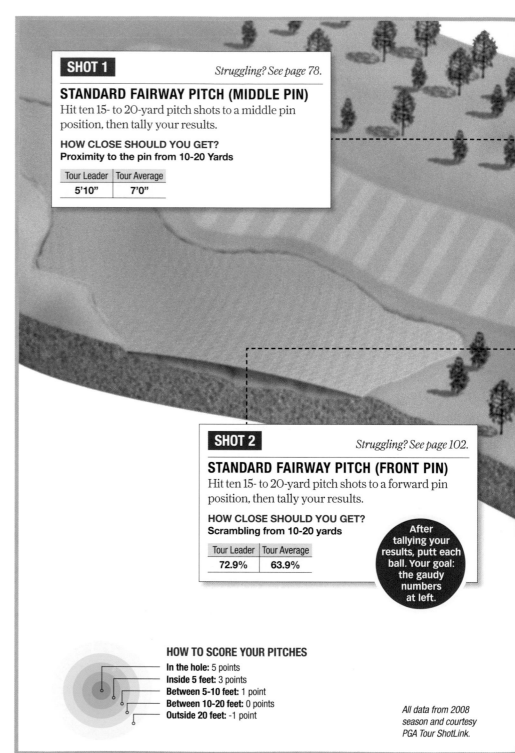

SHOT 1   *Struggling? See page 78.*

STANDARD FAIRWAY PITCH (MIDDLE PIN)

Hit ten 15- to 20-yard pitch shots to a middle pin position, then tally your results.

HOW CLOSE SHOULD YOU GET?
Proximity to the pin from 10-20 Yards

Tour Leader	Tour Average
5'10"	7'0"

SHOT 2   *Struggling? See page 102.*

STANDARD FAIRWAY PITCH (FRONT PIN)

Hit ten 15- to 20-yard pitch shots to a forward pin position, then tally your results.

HOW CLOSE SHOULD YOU GET?
Scrambling from 10-20 yards

Tour Leader	Tour Average
72.9%	63.9%

After tallying your results, putt each ball. Your goal: the gaudy numbers at left.

HOW TO SCORE YOUR PITCHES

In the hole: 5 points
Inside 5 feet: 3 points
Between 5-10 feet: 1 point
Between 10-20 feet: 0 points
Outside 20 feet: -1 point

All data from 2008 season and courtesy PGA Tour ShotLink.

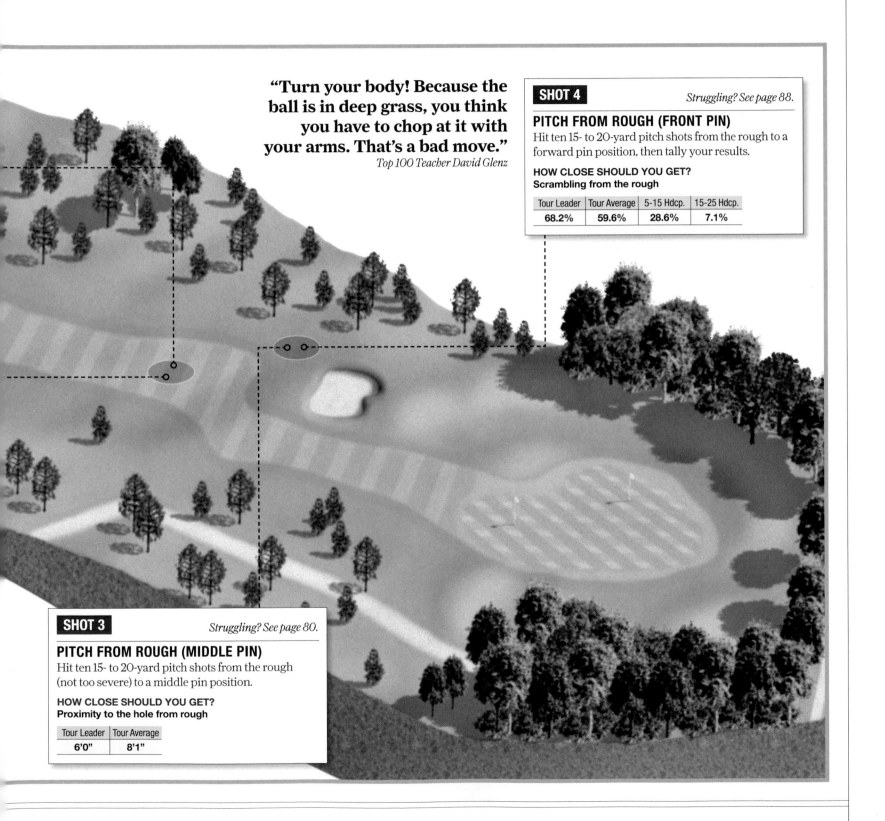

"**Turn your body! Because the ball is in deep grass, you think you have to chop at it with your arms. That's a bad move.**"
Top 100 Teacher David Glenz

SHOT 4   *Struggling? See page 88.*

PITCH FROM ROUGH (FRONT PIN)

Hit ten 15- to 20-yard pitch shots from the rough to a forward pin position, then tally your results.

HOW CLOSE SHOULD YOU GET?
Scrambling from the rough

Tour Leader	Tour Average	5-15 Hdcp.	15-25 Hdcp.
68.2%	59.6%	28.6%	7.1%

SHOT 3   *Struggling? See page 80.*

PITCH FROM ROUGH (MIDDLE PIN)

Hit ten 15- to 20-yard pitch shots from the rough (not too severe) to a middle pin position.

HOW CLOSE SHOULD YOU GET?
Proximity to the hole from rough

Tour Leader	Tour Average
6'0"	8'1"

Rate Your Chip Shots

TAKE THE TEST!

Head out to the course and find a hole with a varied green complex. Look for a slightly elevated green with collection areas off to the sides. It's okay if the green is significantly sloped—give yourself a bit of a challenge on this one. (Again, build this hole in your mind if you're performing this test at the range, or try it on the practice chipping green.) Hit 10 balls from each of the stations pictured at right, scoring them using the Shot Rating Guide on the opposite page. Then use the table below to tally your results and see where your wedge game is in need of the most help.

ADD IT UP
Tally the results of each test using the scorecard at right.

	FAIRWAY CHIP	FLOP SHOT	CHIP FROM FRINGE	SHORT-SIDED CHIP
#1				
#2				
#3				
#4				
#5				
#6				
#7				
#8				
#9				
#10				
TOTAL				

RATING SCALE: ACE > 25 **SOLID** 20-25 **FAIR** 15-20 **OUCH** < 15

SHOT 1 *Struggling? See page 106.*

CHIP FROM THE FAIRWAY

Hit 10 medium-length chips from a nice lie in the fairway, then tally your results.

HOW CLOSE SHOULD YOU GET?
Proximity to the hole <10 yards

Tour Leader	Tour Average
2'7"	3'8"

From short range your goal is to chip the ball into tap-in range every time.

SHOT 2 *Struggling? See page 175.*

FLOP SHOT

Hit 10 flops. After tallying your results, hole each putt, and see how close you get to the numbers below.

HOW CLOSE SHOULD YOU GET?
Scrambling < 10 Yards

Tour Leader	Tour Average
94.5%	84.7%

HOW TO SCORE YOUR CHIPS
In the hole: 5 points
Inside 3 feet: 3 points
Between 3-6 feet: 1 point
Between 6-10 feet: 0 points
Outside 10 feet: -1 point

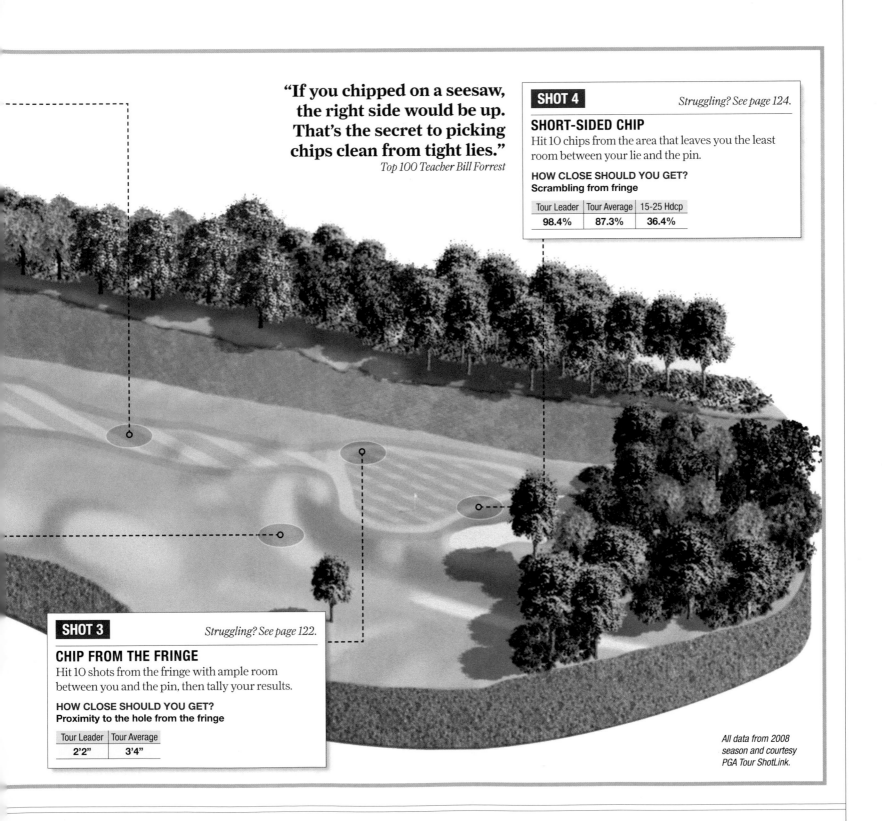

"If you chipped on a seesaw, the right side would be up. That's the secret to picking chips clean from tight lies."

Top 100 Teacher Bill Forrest

SHOT 4

Struggling? See page 124.

SHORT-SIDED CHIP

Hit 10 chips from the area that leaves you the least room between your lie and the pin.

HOW CLOSE SHOULD YOU GET?
Scrambling from fringe

Tour Leader	Tour Average	15-25 Hdcp
98.4%	87.3%	36.4%

SHOT 3

Struggling? See page 122.

CHIP FROM THE FRINGE

Hit 10 shots from the fringe with ample room between you and the pin, then tally your results.

HOW CLOSE SHOULD YOU GET?
Proximity to the hole from the fringe

Tour Leader	Tour Average
2'2"	3'4"

All data from 2008 season and courtesy PGA Tour ShotLink.

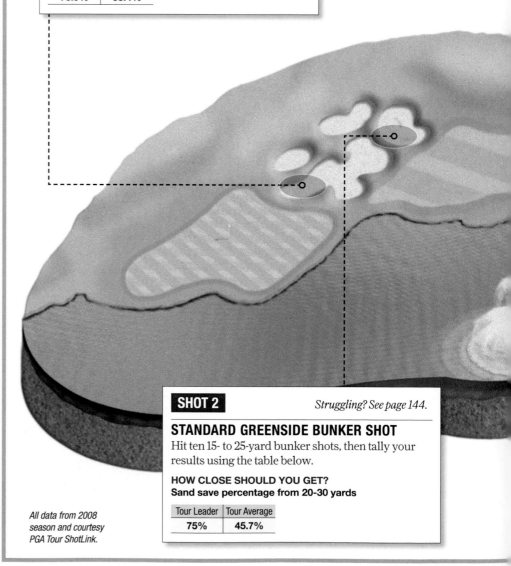

HOW TO

Rate Your Bunker Shots

TAKE THE TEST!

For this test, find a hole with several standard greenside bunkers—we won't ask you to test your game out of a pot bunker or nasty waster area. Also, make sure the designer has placed a bunker at that tricky 40-yard distance from the green. If you're performing this drill at the range, use any practice bunker and imagine the different distances. Hit 10 balls from each of the stations pictured at right, scoring them using the Shot Rating Guide on the opposite page. Use the table below to tally your results and see where your wedge game is in need of the most help.

ADD IT UP
Tally the results of each test using the scorecard at right.

	BUNKER CHIP (10 YARDS TO GREEN CENTER)	BUNKER CHIP (20 YARDS TO GREEN CENTER)	BUNKER CHIP (40 YARDS TO GREEN CENTER)
#1			
#2			
#3			
#4			
#5			
#6			
#7			
#8			
#9			
#10			
TOTAL			

RATING SCALE: ACE > 15   **SOLID** 10-15   **FAIR** 0-10   **OUCH** < 0

SHOT 1   *Struggling? See page 138.*

SHORT GREENSIDE BUNKER SHOT
Hit ten 10- to 15-yard bunker shots, then tally your results using the table below.

HOW CLOSE SHOULD YOU GET?
Sand save percentage from 10-20 yards

Tour Leader	Tour Average
73.9%	53.4%

> **"On most bunker shots, the first thing that should enter the sand is the trailing edge."**
> *Top 100 Teacher Mike Malaska*

SHOT 2   *Struggling? See page 144.*

STANDARD GREENSIDE BUNKER SHOT
Hit ten 15- to 25-yard bunker shots, then tally your results using the table below.

HOW CLOSE SHOULD YOU GET?
Sand save percentage from 20-30 yards

Tour Leader	Tour Average
75%	45.7%

All data from 2008 season and courtesy PGA Tour ShotLink.

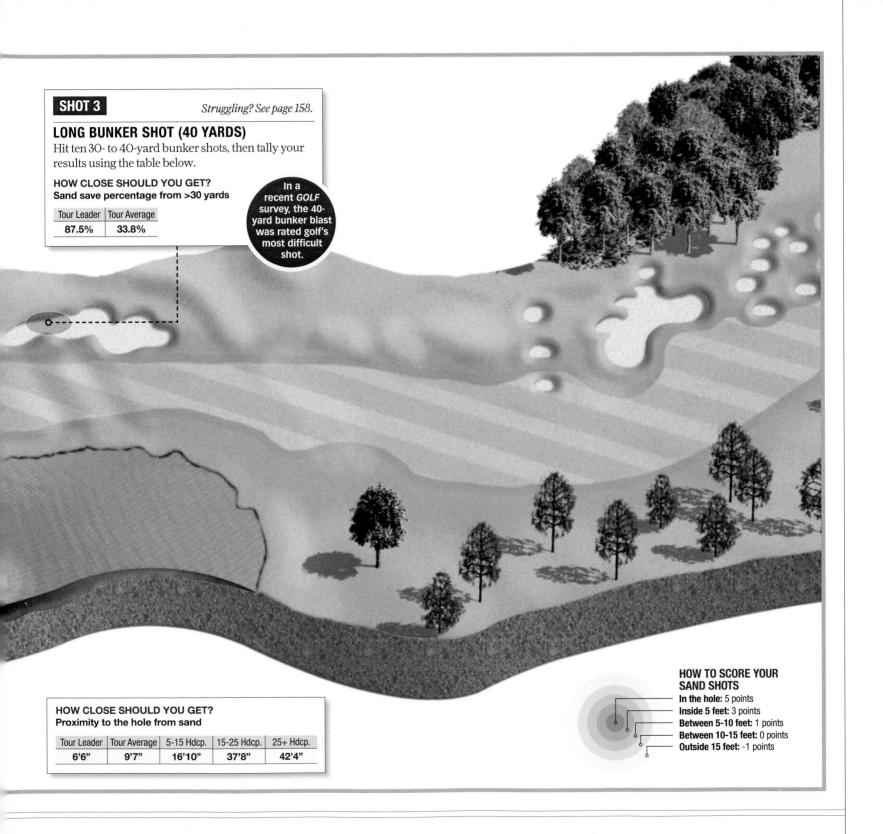

SHOT 3

Struggling? See page 158.

LONG BUNKER SHOT (40 YARDS)

Hit ten 30- to 40-yard bunker shots, then tally your results using the table below.

HOW CLOSE SHOULD YOU GET?
Sand save percentage from >30 yards

Tour Leader	Tour Average
87.5%	33.8%

In a recent *GOLF* survey, the 40-yard bunker blast was rated golf's most difficult shot.

HOW CLOSE SHOULD YOU GET?
Proximity to the hole from sand

Tour Leader	Tour Average	5-15 Hdcp.	15-25 Hdcp.	25+ Hdcp.
6'6"	9'7"	16'10"	37'8"	42'4"

HOW TO SCORE YOUR SAND SHOTS
In the hole: 5 points
Inside 5 feet: 3 points
Between 5-10 feet: 1 points
Between 10-15 feet: 0 points
Outside 15 feet: -1 points

HOW TO

Rate Your Round

A new tracking system tells you instantly where your scoring went awry

—Top 100 Teacher Jerry Mowlds

THIS STORY IS FOR YOU IF...

1 You hit good shots during the round you just finished...

2 ...but you can't understand how you scored so poorly.

TRY THIS!

The next time you play, keep a second scorecard. Label each row with "Putts, Shot 1, Shot 2, Shot 3, Shot 4," etc. Mark the score box for each shot to indicate the club used, whether or not you hit the fairway or green (X for hit, O for miss), the direction of your misses (with an arrow) and the quality of your contact ("3" for excellent contact, "2" for okay contact and "1" for poor contact). When you get to the green, write down the number of putts and the distance of your first and any remaining putts (see the card at right).

WHY IT WORKS

There are numerous score- and stat-tracking programs you can use to evaluate your game, but very few of them give you an indication of the quality of your ballstriking like this simple method. (You can still hit the fairway with a drop-kick skull off the tee). Plus, this tracking system provides you with instant feedback on the round you just played and holds the clues as to why you posted the score you wrote on your other card.

HOW TO FILL OUT YOUR CARD

Fairway/green hit: **X**
Fairway/green missed: **O**
Excellent contact: **3**
Okay contact: **2**
Poor contact: **1**
First-putt distance/second-putt distance: **24/12**
Clubs: **3w, 5w, 3h, 3i, 4i...**

GHOST CREEK

					HDCP	PAR
1	328	372	392	447	9	4
2	325	364	391	414	11	4
3	108	128	158	184	17	3
4	414	495	515	533	1	5
5	179	193	205	218	13	3
6	316	341	366	371	15	4
7	301	384	409	431	7	4
8	462	497	562	573	5	5
9	368	419	443	469	3	4
Out	2801	3193	3441	3640		36
10	410	453	474	492	6	5
11	122	145	170	180	16	3
12	327	370	406	444	8	4
13	295	329	356	381	10	4
14	167	201	219	234	14	3
15	421	498	531	552	2	5
16	97	113	125	133	18	3
17	224	273	301	329	4	4
18	342	381	428	454	12	4
In	2405	2763	3010	3199		35
Total	5206	5956	6451	6839		71
			71.9	73.8	HDCP	
		69.0			NET	
				140	POST	

QUALITY METER

Scan the contact ratings of your first and second shots. If you see mostly 1s and 2s, you know that the quality of your strikes kept you from playing your best. Focus on improving contact during your next practice session.

ACCURACY METER

Scan the fairways- and greens-hit markings. If you see that you hit a lot of accurate shots but posted a higher-than-normal score, look to your putting stats. If you see mostly Os and not Xs, then you know your troubles came from hitting inaccurate drives and approaches.

SHORT-GAME METER

When you miss a green, check the distance of your first putt in the putting column. It's a quick way to gauge the quality of your short game and whether you're wasting strokes by chipping and pitching to distances beyond your comfortable two-putt range.

PUTTING METER

If you see mostly 1s and 2s in the putting row, congratulations! Odds are you posted a decent score. If a few 3s pop up, however, check the numbers on the distance of your first putts and the ones that followed. If many of your first putts were from distances greater than 20 feet, then you know that your three-putting was the result of not getting your approaches and wedge shots close enough to the hole. If the second numbers are higher than 4, then you know you three-putted because you didn't get your first stroke close enough for a two-putt.

Chipping a ball over your bag without touching it with your sand wedge is an easy way to build chip distance control so you don't leave yourself a lengthy first putt.

How to Make Your First Putt Shorter

BONUS TIP: If your putting numbers indicate you're not getting your short shots close enough to the hole for a two-putt, try this drill. Lay your bag down about 18 inches in front of your ball. Address the ball with your sand wedge, and keep your weight shifted forward and your hands ahead of the ball. Make your normal chipping stroke so that the ball clears the bag but the clubhead doesn't touch the bag. The bag forces you to make a sharp, descending blow with plenty of acceleration. This stroke puts spin on the ball, which gives you more control of the speed on the green so you don't come up short or chip the ball too far.

> "If many of your first putts were from distances greater than 20 feet, then you know that your three-putting was the result of not getting your approaches and wedge shots close enough to the hole." —Top 100 Teacher Jerry Mowlds

Good wedge players pounce on pins from 100 yards and in. Their secret: a swing that favors contact and control over speed.

4

STIFF YOUR WEDGE SHOTS

How to dominate from 100 yards and in with full, half and specialty wedge swings

GET HOT IN THE RED ZONE

You're within 100 yards of the pin. Now isn't the time to think about getting on—it's the time to think about getting *close*, even from those tricky in-between distances when you can't make a full swing with one of your wedges.

The secret to hitting short approaches is to strip your swing down to its basic roots, and keep everything connected. You use the shortest clubs in your bag for these shots, which means your swing should favor control over speed and power. Save the miles per hour for your driver, woods and irons, and focus on making centered contact with the clubface pointing at your target. You'll find all the advice you need to do exactly that on the following pages, plus surefire ways to adjust your motion to generate the right distance to any flag.

You'll make an immediate improvement in your game if you learn to consistently produce shots that fly 100, 75 and 50 yards. Getting these distances down pat allows you to land the ball close from a variety of other wedge distances.

TECHNIQUE

Hit 100-, 75- and 50-yard Approach Shots

Nailing these yardages makes you laser-accurate from every distance in between

—Top 100 Teacher Mark Hackett

THE SITUATION

You piped your drive on a short par 4, or hit an excellent layup shot on a par 5, and are sitting within easy wedge distance of the pin. There's nothing better than staring down the flag from short range, unless you don't know how hard to swing—or which wedge to pull from your bag—to hit the ball the correct distance to the hole.

THE SOLUTION

Over the course of a year you'll face dozens of different distances to the pin from short range. If you're serious about your game, you'll eventually need to learn how to control your swing to hit very specific yardages with each one of your wedges *[see page 74]*. In the meantime, it's a good idea to learn how to land the ball close from 100, 75 and 50 yards. You'll find that the majority of your wedge shots take place from somewhere near these benchmark distances. All you need are three clubs and three very similar swings. Turn the page to learn how to groove them.

TOP 100 TEACHER POLL

Q What's the most important part about hitting wedge approach shots?

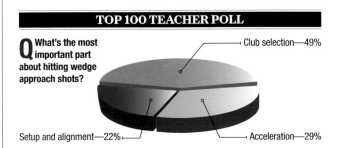

Club selection—49%
Acceleration—29%
Setup and alignment—22%

"You have 14 clubs in your bag, and at least four should be wedges. When you pick the right wedge, hitting the correct distance becomes very easy."—Top 100 Teacher Jon Tattersall

HOW TO

Hit It 100 Yards

Make it a full swing with a full follow-through
—Top 100 Teacher Mark Hackett

DO THIS!

In order to consistently generate that magical 100-yard distance (you'll be surprised how often you find yourself at this yardage), you need to discover which club gets you closest to the number. For most golfers, that's a pitching wedge or a gap wedge. The next time you're at the range, empty a half-bucket of balls using just these two clubs, and check which one gets you on the 100-yard marker the most. One of them will do a better job than the other.

THEN THIS!

Once you have your 100-yard club, follow the steps at right to make sure you hit it crisp, clean and on the number when you're on the course. The secret is to take advantage of the fact you can make a full swing.

> **"The secret to hitting a 100-yard shot is to take advantage of the fact you can make a full swing."**

ON THE NUMBER

Q **How close do PGA Tour pros get it from 100 yards?**

🟦 Tour average 🟩 Tour leader

Data courtesy PGA Tour ShotLink

PROXIMITY TO THE HOLE FROM 100-125 YARDS

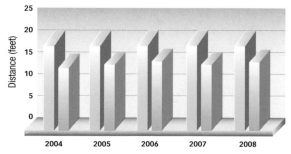

Distance (feet)	2004	2005	2006	2007	2008

Most Tour pros leave 100-yard shots about 20 feet from the hole, while the best in the world get it five feet closer on average. What's more impressive is their consistency—they hit the number almost every time.

STEP 1: SET IT UP

Copy the positions here to set up a perfect full swing with your 100-yard club. You can vary ball position, stance width and stance angle to tweak the distance, but keep these fundamentals intact when you're dead on the number.

HANDS
Set your hands so that the shaft points at the center of your body. You don't have to lean the shaft forward like you see some golfers do.

STANCE
Take a hip-width stance. Anything narrower locks the turning action of your hips (not good).

BALL
Position the ball in the middle of your stance.

GRIP
Grip on the top of the handle. No choke needed here.

CLUBFACE
Point your clubface at your target. Open faces lead to missed greens.

STANCE
Set your feet toe to toe. If you drop your left foot back or flare it, you'll inhibit your shoulder turn and power, causing you to come up short of your target.

STEP 2: SWING FULL-TO-FULL

Your square-toe, hip-width stance allows you to turn your shoulders and hips freely during your backswing. Although it's a short shot, you need this turning power or you won't generate the full distance of the club in your hands.

STEP 3: KEEP IT CONNECTED

Notice how my shoulders and hips have unwound at almost the same pace. You don't see the wide-open hips normally associated with driver impact. It's good to think about moving everything—your shoulders, hips, arms and clubhead—together when swinging a full wedge.

STEP 4: DON'T STOP

When you're firing at the pin from short range, it's easy to peek too early to see where your ball is headed. Stay down through the shot and swing to a full, complete finish, just like you do with your woods.

You know you've made a solid 100-yard wedge swing if you end your swing with a complete finish and in total balance. Notice that I've only slightly raised my right heel—it's not way up like it is when I'm swinging driver. It's a good idea to feel a little flat-footed when swinging your wedge to help with your control.

The 100-Yard Swing

Copy the positions here
for balance and control
—*Top 100 Teacher Mark Hackett*

A ONE-PIECE MOTION

The biggest thing to draw from
this sequence is how the arms
match the body—everything is
moving in concert. As I turn my
shoulders and hips, my arms and
hands follow right along. Nothing
jumps too far ahead or lags too
far behind. Keeping your swing
connected like this on both sides
of the ball allows you to stay in
balance and control the club
through impact. If it looks easy, it's
because it is. Think of making a
smooth backswing, then gradually
accelerating into the ball.

> "The most
> important thing
> is to make your
> swing the same
> size on both sides
> of the ball."

1

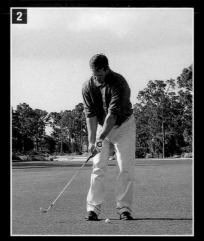

2

3
Shoulders slightly
lead the turning
action of the hips.

8
It's an arms,
shoulders
and hips
swing.

9
Like all swings,
the downswing
starts by
bumping your
left hip toward
the target.

10

15

16
Impact looks
very similar to
setup. Weight is
forward so club
swings down
into the ball.

17

6 Full, 90-degree set of the wrists.

12 Everything unwinds together.

14 Momentum releases the hinge in your wrists.

18 Gradual deceleration into a balanced, full finish.

HOW TO
Hit It 75 Yards

The secret to getting this one close is all in your wrist hinge
—*Top 100 Teacher Mark Hackett*

DO THIS!
Like you did for the 100-yard wedge shot, hit the range and empty a half-bucket of balls and see which of your wedges consistently gets you to 75 yards. Don't make giant, full swings; focus on smoothly accelerating the club from the top of a three-quarter backswing. What you'll find is that the 75-yard distance falls right between your sand wedge and lob wedge.

THEN THIS!
Since it's difficult to add yards to a club without it affecting your swing, opt for your sand wedge, and make the setup adjustments at right. These easy address changes automatically shorten your swing, so you take just enough yards off your sand iron to hit the 75-yard number.

> "A narrower stance decreases the amount you can comfortably turn your body, taking yards off your swing."

ON THE NUMBER

Q How close do PGA Tour pros get it from 75 to 100 yards?

■ Tour average ■ Tour leader
Data courtesy PGA Tour ShotLink

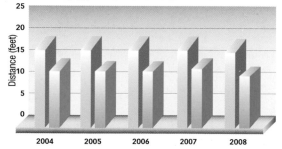

PROXIMITY TO THE HOLE FROM 75-100 YARDS

Distance (feet) — 2004, 2005, 2006, 2007, 2008

The best wedge players in the world knock it extra-tight from this distance. Even better, they land it in the range when Tour players begin to start sinking a majority of their first putts (10 to 12 feet).

STEP 1: SET IT UP
Copy the positions here to set up a perfect three-quarter swing with your sand wedge (i.e., the one that will consistently hit the ball 75 yards).

STANCE
Take a shoulder-width stance. A narrower stance makes it harder to turn your body (a good thing when you're trying to shorten your swing).

HANDS
Set your hands so that the shaft points at the center of your body. Since the ball is slightly back you should see the shaft leaning toward the target.

BALL
Position the ball slightly behind the middle of your stance.

GRIP
Grip slightly down on the handle, toward the middle. This is another easy way to take yards off your swing.

CLUBFACE
Point your clubface at your target, just like you did for the 100-yard shot (and like you'll do for the 50-yard shot and every wedge approach in between).

STANCE
Pull your left foot back so that your left toe is even with the ball of your right foot. This left-foot pull back makes it slightly more difficult to turn your shoulders all the way back.

STEP 2: SWING THREE-QUARTER TO THREE-QUARTER

Your toe-to-ball, shoulder-width stance limits your shoulder and hip flexibility, making it easy to stop your swing at three-quarters back. This is the backswing distance that will most frequently generate 75 yards with your sand wedge.

STEP 3: CONSTANT ACCELERATION

When swings stop short of full, golfers make the mistake of swinging with less-than-full energy on the way back down, or pulling the club violently into impact. Get comfortable with a shorter backswing, and smoothly accelerate as if you were hitting the shot full.

STEP 4: MATCH SWING LENGTHS

Since you stopped at three-quarters back, finish at three-quarters through. This happens almost automatically because of your narrow stance. If you try to swing to a full finish, you'll likely fall off balance.

Although you shorten your backswing to hit the ball 75 yards, don't cut your wrist hinge. You need the same 90-degree hinge you use on full swings. A solid hinge is needed to add energy to your motion, and to hit the ball on a high trajectory so that it can fly all the way to your target.

The 75-Yard Swing

Less turn and your usual hinge make it happen

—*Top 100 Teacher Mark Hackett*

SHORTER, BUT PACKED WITH POWER

When you narrow your stance, you lose hip flexibility. (Try it now—stand up, put your feet together and try to rotate your hips in a mock backswing. See what I mean?) This restricted hip movement automatically shortens every part of your motion. The major mistake to avoid is over-swinging your arms after your hips and shoulders have stopped turning. Once you feel your hands reach chest height, it's time to swing back down.

"The major mistake to avoid is over-swinging your arms after your hips have stopped turning."

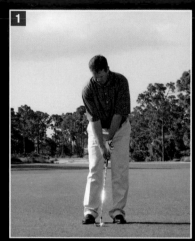

1

2

3

Less hip turn due to narrower stance.

8

9

10

Head holding steady over ball.

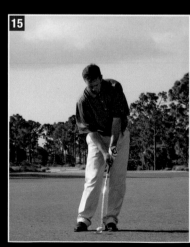

15

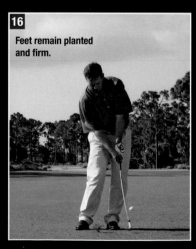

16

Feet remain planted and firm.

17

4

5 Club hinges earlier than in a full swing.

6

7 No real weight shift (actually favors left foot).

11

12

13 Belt line is horizontal—left hip turning, not lifting.

14

18

19

20 Slight right ankle roll to complete the weight shift.

21 Finish matches backswing.

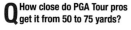

Hit It 50 Yards

You only need half a swing to get
50-yarders to tap-in range
—*Top 100 Teacher Mark Hackett*

DO THIS!

With even your shortest and most-lofted wedge (likely a lob wedge), you're going to hit the ball farther than 50 yards with a smooth, solid, full swing. Most golfers can squeeze 60 to 70 yards out of the lobber. Hit the range and see if your lob shots fall within this range if you don't already know how far you

hit your L-wedge. (If you don't have an L-wedge, get one this weekend). All you need to do is shave 10 to 15 yards off this club. You'll do it with your setup, just like you did for the 75-yard shot.

THEN THIS!

Take the setup changes you made for the 75-yard shot a step further to shorten your swing even that much more, and hit that 50-yard distance on the number. With the setup changes listed at right, you're treading into pitch-shot territory. You should be able to get this one real close nine times out of ten.

> "Control distance with your setup, not your swing."

ON THE NUMBER

Q How close do PGA Tour pros get it from 50 to 75 yards?

■ Tour average ■ Tour leader
Data courtesy PGA Tour ShotLink

PROXIMITY TO THE HOLE FROM 50-75 YARDS

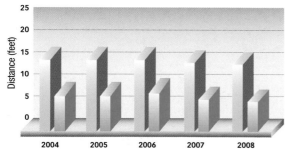

For the average Tour pro, anything outside of 15 feet from 50 to 75 yards is a mistake. How much better would you score if you could get shots from these distances within 10 feet of the pin? That's where the best in the world land them for easy up-and-downs.

STEP 1: SET IT UP

Copy the positions here to set up a pitch-type swing with your lob wedge and knock it stiff from 50 yards every time.

HANDS
Set your hands so that the shaft points at the center of your body. Since your stance is so narrow, the shaft should lean only slightly toward the target.

STANCE
Set your feet about a club's width apart. This will give you almost zero hip turn.

BALL
Position the ball slightly behind the middle of your stance.

GRIP
Grip your lob wedge in the middle of the handle.

CLUBFACE
Point your clubface at your target—the constant among all wedge shots from the fairway.

STANCE
Pull your left foot back so that your left toe is even with the instep of your right foot. Doing this will severely limit your shoulder turn, making your 50-yard swing mostly arms.

STEP 2: MAKE A HALF-BACKSWING

Your toe-to-instep, ultra-narrow stance severely limits your shoulder and hip flexibility, making it easy to stop your swing at halfway back. This is the backswing distance that will consistently produce 50 yards with your sand wedge.

STEP 3: FOCUS ON CONTACT

Forget about what's happening in your backswing and concentrate on what you need to do on your way back down. This is a small swing, so your main goal is to make sure you come down sharply on the back of the ball. You'll know you did it right if you make an audible "click" at impact.

STEP 4: MATCH SWING LENGTHS

Since you stopped at halfway back, finish at halfway through. This happens almost automatically because of your ultra-narrow stance.

Cut your follow-through at hip height, with your hips and shoulders pointing slightly right of your target. The club should feel light in your hands—this is more of a momentum swing than a power swing. Also, stay flat-footed through the shot. Since your hips don't turn as much for a 50-yard swing, there's no need to raise up on your right toe.

The 50-Yard Swing

Get this one right and you'll score like a pro
—*Top 100 Teacher Mark Hackett*

USE YOUR ARMS TO KNOCK IT CLOSE

There's a reason you see most professionals narrow their stances when hitting approach shots from short distance: a narrower stance fuels a shorter, more controlled backswing. What gives this shot its oomph is a slight wrist hinge—you still need to cock the club up even though you're making only half of a backswing. From there, it's just a matter of swinging your arms back down, releasing the hinge, and putting a clean, solid strike on the ball. Your finish is of little consequence.

> "A narrower stance fuels a shorter, more controlled backswing."

1 Feet set a club's width apart.

2 An arms-dominated takeaway.

3

8 A short arm swing, but plenty of wrist hinge. Think "low hands, high clubhead."

9

10

15 A touch of knees adds smoothness.

16 Shoulders and hips slowly unwind—you should feel square at impact.

17

4

5 Shoulders and hips turn, but much less than they do in a standard swing.

6

7

11 Arms swing down while wrists release their hinge.

12

13

14 Fairly quiet lower body.

18

19

20 Right knee kicking slightly toward the target, but a fairly even weight distribution.

21

SINGLE MOTION

The most striking thing about this picture is how together everything looks—if Sergio repeated this look on every wedge swing he'd be hard to beat. There's a sense that everything—hips, shoulders, hands and clubhead—are moving together as a single unit. That's a great feeling to have with your wedge.

QUIET BODY

Solid wedge strikes aren't power strikes—you don't need lots of leg and hip action to hit crisp short shots. When pros hit wedges, they're noticeably flat-footed through impact—they simply make a nice turn back and through the ball. Whereas you'd be hard-pressed to empty a bucket of range balls with your driver, you should be able to hit wedge shots all day without growing tired.

NATURAL ROTATION

A big part of keeping everything connected in your wedge swing, and smoothly accelerating into impact, is to allow for the natural rotation of your forearms. Feel the club rotating open in your takeaway, so that the toe points at the sky halfway back, and reverse the process through impact, so that the toe points to the sky on the target side of your swing. This gives you a smooth, accelerating release.

Sergio Garcia

When people talk about Sergio Garcia's game, the topic usually centers around his incredible clubhead lag, and his ability to hit pure, clean iron shots. But what has helped him to become more competitive—especially in majors and in the bigger tournaments on Tour—is his ever-increasing skill from short range. Like most young players, Sergio hadn't learned to hit consistent short shots into greens when he first began competing on the professional circuit. Since 2001, however, he's increased his greens-hit-in-regulation percentage from less than 100 yards every season. His short game is helping him rise—and remain—at the top.

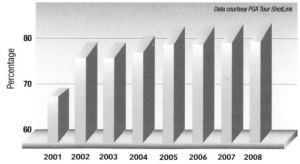

G.I.R. PERCENTAGE FROM <125 YARDS

Data courtesy PGA Tour ShotLink

Percentage: 80, 70, 60

2001 2002 2003 2004 2005 2006 2007 2008

Garcia has improved his G.I.R. percentage from short range every year since 2001.

Hit a Punch Shot

Why take a full swing when a half-swing gets you home just as easily?

—Top 100 Teacher Anne Cain

THIS STORY IS FOR YOU IF...

1
You're not a strong iron or wedge player.

2
You often play in windy conditions.

THE SITUATION

You're a solid pitching wedge from the green, but you have to put your absolute best swing on the ball to get it near the pin. How often does that happen?

THE SMART PLAY

The longer the backswing, the less margin for error, yet most golfers select a club based on a full swing for the yardage at hand. This is a huge strategical mistake, especially when you can get away with swinging a longer club a little shorter. These "punch" shots are a shotmaker's best friend, especially when the green is open, or when the wind is blowing (the punch's lower trajectory negates the effects of wind).

HOW TO PUNCH IT LOW AND CLOSE

STEP 1
Keep everything the same, but stop your backswing when your hands reach chest high. Make sure you've hinged your wrists fully, with the clubhead high above your hands. From the top, turn through the ball like normal.

STEP 2
Keep your clubhead low to the ground after impact—this helps the ball fly low and shoot out with a more piercing trajectory. Finishing low also reduces the chances of swiping across the ball and hitting a cut. If you select the right club for the distance you're facing *[see chart]*, you'll end up in perfect shape on the green.

Use this yardage guide to pull the right club when you elect to make a punch-shot swing.

Club	Full-Swing Distance	Punch-Swing Distance
7-iron	165 yards	130 yards
8-iron	150 yards	115 yards
9-iron	135 yards	100 yards
PW	125 yards	85 yards

Swing Left to Hit It Straight

Swing your arms left after impact so you don't push short shots to the right
—Top 100 Teacher Martin Hall

THE PROBLEM

No matter what you try, you never make great contact with your wedges. They feel a little thin, and you rarely generate spin or the right trajectory.

THE SOLUTION

When you have a wedge in your hand, you're making a small, controlled swing with the shortest club in your bag and the target sitting ultra-close. Because of this, you're tempted to steer the ball toward the flag by swinging down the target line. That's a recipe for disaster. Just like you do with your longer clubs, it's important to continue your body turn after impact and swing the club to the left of the target. Swinging left like this gives you a more solid strike, and is what actually makes the ball fly straight.

When you swing to the left of the target after impact, the ball tends to fly straight.

A TIP THAT WORKS
Imagine that you're swinging in front of a wall (picture your rear end touching it at impact). As you swing into your follow-through, try to slap the wall with your right hand. That will help you keep your swing on plane and hit the kind of crisp wedges that get you close.

THIS STORY IS FOR YOU IF...

1
You hit your wedges solid, but to the right.

2
You'd score a lot better if you hit your wedges a few yards closer to the pin.

TRY THIS!

Swing your wedges at 90 percent

Players looking for more power tend to try to stretch a few extra yards out of their clubs. In some cases, it's a smart move. Taking a more aggressive attitude with a fairway wood or mid-iron can produce excellent results. But when it comes to your wedges, it's definitely a bad idea.

Longer clubs, such as your driver, create a lot of centrifugal force during your swing. Your body responds to and supports that force. As a result, if you try to lay into the driver, you create enough centrifugal force to keep your body in good position during the swing. But since the shaft on your wedge is almost a foot shorter than your driver, it creates much less centrifugal force during your swing. As a result, your body does not respond as well to high swing speeds with the shorter club.

Swing too hard with a wedge and your body tends to slide out of position, resulting in poor contact or errant shots. Remember that wedge shots are all about accuracy; don't try to swing harder than 90 percent. If that isn't enough to get you to your target, take more club. You'll get better results by swinging easier.

The short shaft of the wedge creates much less centrifugal force, and when you swing too hard your body slides out of position. Don't swing harder than 90 percent.

STRATEGY

Make Six Easy Pars with Your Wedges

Play to your go-to-approach distance to make simple work of par 5s and short par 4s

—Top 100 Teacher Kellie Stenzel

THIS STORY IS FOR YOU IF...

1
You never know what to do with your second shot on a par 5.

2
You almost always take the longest club and try to hit it out of the park.

THE SITUATION

You're in the middle of the fairway on a par 5 (and far enough from the green to nix any thoughts of going for the green in two), or on the tee box of a short par 4. Sure, hitting the longest club you can find and getting as close to the green as possible sounds like a good idea, but that introduces yet another long swing into your round, and possibly the need to hit a trick shot into the green from an unfamiliar distance.

THE SMART PLAY

Whenever you're at a distance outside the range of your longest club, hit whatever iron gets you to your most comfortable distance from the green. For some, it could be 125 yards; other golfers may feel more comfortable hitting a 75-yard approach. There's no correct answer: everyone has a "go-to" wedge distance.

For example, if you're 225 yards from the green, and you tend to hit your sand wedge 75 yards on the money almost every time, then hit your 150-yard club. (Same goes for short par 4s: If the hole measure 340 yards, then hit your 190-yard club off the tee). This sets you up to hit the flagstick on your very next shot.

ON THE NUMBER

Q How often do Tour players go for par-5 greens in two instead of laying up?

Data courtesy PGA Tour ShotLink

Professionals are going for par-5 greens in two less and less frequently, in part because courses are getting longer, and also because the scoring benefits provided by laying up to a go-to wedge distance are very real.

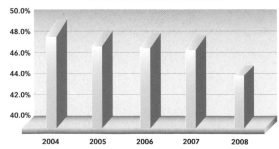

GOING FOR THE GREEN PERCENTAGE

50.0%
48.0%
46.0%
44.0%
42.0%
40.0%

2004   2005   2006   2007   2008

HOW TO FIND YOUR GO-TO APPROACH

Hit the range and smack a dozen balls each with your sand wedge, pitching wedge and your 9-iron (hit your 8-iron, too, just in case), and simply look at the results. Check both the dispersion pattern and the consistency in distance. The distance at which you produced the tightest grouping is the distance you should lay up to on par 5s and drive to on short par 4s.

With this number in mind, play for position as well as distance when you're on the course. Look for approach angles that avoid the need to carry hazards or trouble. For example, if the pin is cut deep left behind a bunker, then lay-up to the right side of the fairway so you'll have an unobstructed path to the pin.

STROKE SAVER

Learn to shape shots to attack any pin placement

For most players, any decision on what club to hit from around 100 yards starts and ends with sand wedge. That's not the best way to post the lowest number possible on your scorecard. Good players may often hit sand wedge from that distance, but only if the situation calls for it. If the pin is back, for example, a high-level player is more likely to hit a longer club lower and short of the hole and let the ball run up to the flag. For any given short shot, a good wedge player should have five basic ways to get the ball close [see illustration]. Each of these plays give you the best chance to knock the ball close without risking hitting into trouble.

Work on creating these five basic shot shapes, and you'll be able to attack whatever pin position the greenskeeper throws at you. At the very least, learn how to hit the ball 100 yards with a high trajectory and with a low trajectory. To hit the ball higher, simply make your normal swing. There's enough loft on your short irons and wedges to get the job done. Producing a lower ballflight is just as easy, and you have three ways you can do it. You can swing a longer club easier, choke down, or play the ball back. Also, you can subscribe to the old rule that a lower finish results in a lower shot. Try chopping off your follow-through when your hands reach shoulder height.

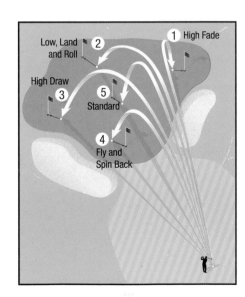

Stick Wedge Shots From The Rough

A more vertical swing gets you through the junk and on the green
—Top 100 Teacher Mark Hackett

THE SITUATION
Good news—you're within easy wedge distance of the green. Bad news—your ball is sitting in rough. Most of the ball is visible, but there's just enough grass between it and the clubface to make you think twice about what you need to do.

THE SMART PLAY
Hitting in the rough is a definite penalty. Whenever grass gets between the ball and the clubface, you tend to lose spin. If the blades are long enough, you'll lose speed and directional control as well. The secret is to minimize the time the clubhead spends in contact with the grass before impact. You can do this by making a slightly more vertical swing. Follow the cues at right.

ON THE NUMBER

Q How difficult is it to hit wedge shots from the rough close?

☐ Tour average
☐ Tour leader

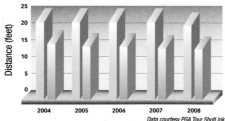

PROXIMITY TO THE HOLE FROM <100 YARDS

Distance (feet): 25, 20, 15, 10, 5, 0

2004   2005   2006   2007   2008

Data courtesy PGA Tour ShotLink

PGA Tour players land wedge approach shots from the fairway approximately 29% closer than those from the rough.

1

THIS STORY IS FOR YOU IF...

1
Hitting from long grass gives you fits...

2
...even when you have a wedge in your hands.

Stand closer to the ball and bend forward more to flatten the shaft angle.

Stand a little closer to the ball and bend slightly more from your hips. This decreases the lie angle of your club.

2

Your stance alterations and flatter shaft angle encourage a steeper backswing swing path.

6

Retrace your vertical backswing on your downswing.

Like all good swings, the hands drop as the hips unwind. Forward bend toward the ball hasn't changed since address.

7

The clubhead traces the same steep descent angle it took going back. The toe of the club is pointing up, just like it should.

Business as usual here: Full set of the wrists, forming a 90-degree angle between your left forearm and the shaft.

Evidence of a vertical path is that the butt of the club points to the grass between your feet and the ball, not at the ball itself.

The flatter shaft angle at address encourages a more vertical backswing.

This is the steepness you need to combat rough. The left arm plane is slightly above the shoulder plane.

The steeper the swing, the less time your clubhead stays in contact with the grass.

Compare the shaft angle here to Frame 1: It's much more vertical at impact. This minimizes grass/clubface interaction.

Notice how the hands swing left of the target after impact, not straight toward the target.

Match your more vertical backswing with a more vertical through-swing.

How to Handle Sloping Lies

Read your lie in the fairway like you do your putts on the green to aim at the right spot

—*Top 100 Teacher Carol Preisinger*

THIS STORY IS FOR YOU IF...

1
You tend to hit your shots on target from flat lies...

2
...but miss way right or left when the ball is above or below your feet.

THE SITUATION

You have a good lie in the fairway about 100 yards from the pin, but the ground is slightly tilted. When you go to take your stance, the ball is either above or below your feet.

THE TYPICAL SOLUTION

Since you've been told that when the ball is above your feet the ball will curve to the left, you aim a few yards right of the pin (and vice versa for when the ball is below your feet). This only gets you close—do you really know how far to aim either left or right of the flagstick?

THE EASY WAY TO ADJUST FOR SLOPE

First, keep in mind that shorter clubs are more affected by slope than longer ones *[see sidebar, opposite page]*, and the distance you need to aim to the left or right is more than you might think. Since you wouldn't just guess on where to aim when facing a breaking putt, why do it here?

When you have a wedge in your hands, treat a sloping lie in the fairway like you do any breaking putt. Get an image of how the shot "breaks," and pick your start line accordingly. You'll hit it much closer to the target than if you just aim slightly left or right. Follow the steps below.

HOW TO PICK THE PERFECT TARGET

STEP 1
Crouch down behind the ball, just like you do when reading putts. Look at the landing area and determine how much a putt from this lie would break to the left (if the ball is above your feet) or to the right (if the ball is below your feet).

STEP 2
Select a target on the green that's on the start line of the putt you'd make from your lie in the fairway. Select a second target that's also on the line, but just in front of where the ball sits in the fairway.

STEP 3
Take your address position using the aiming spot in front of the ball as your reference. The flag is no longer your target—it's the spot you chose either left or right of the pin.

STEP 4

Make your normal everyday motion, being careful to swing along your toe line, not out toward the flagstick. If you played enough "break," the ball will follow its natural curve (to the left when the ball is above your feet, and to the right when the ball is below your feet) and snuggle close to the pin.

FROM THE *GM* VAULT

**How to Knock It Stiff From
A Sidehill Lie**
Top 100 Teacher Bryan Gathright
GOLF Magazine, July 2008

The Adjustment You Need

A sidehill lie with the ball above your feet will cause your ball to curve to the left. But the amount of curve depends on the club in your hands. Because they have more loft and a more upright lie, short irons are more affected by slope than long irons. Because of this difference, you need to aim much farther to the right when you're swinging your wedges and short irons from this lie.

"If you typically use your sand wedge on small pitches and chips and often pull the ball left of the hole, drop down to a less-lofted club, like your pitching wedge or 9-iron."

NEW METHODS

How to Nail Every Distance

My distance-reduction system gives you the power to automatically subtract yards from your club without changing your swing

—*Top 100 Teacher Mike Adams*

THIS STORY IS FOR YOU IF...

1
You often find yourself between clubs from short range and don't know how to adjust.

THE SITUATION

You're in no-mans land—57 yards from the pin. Or maybe you're at 77 yards, or even 46. In other words, you're stuck hard between two wedges and don't know what to do.

THE SOLUTION

Earlier in this chapter you learned how to generate swings to cover the benchmark distances of 100, 75 and 50 yards *[pages 50-63]*. This technique takes you a step further and allows you to remove yards from each of your wedges in very specific increments, making it easy to hit the ball almost every distance from 125 yards and in.

> **"All you have to do is put what you feel is your best full swing on the ball, and your setup does the rest."**

TOP 100 TEACHER POLL

Q When stuck between clubs, should you swing harder with the shorter club or smoother with the longer club?

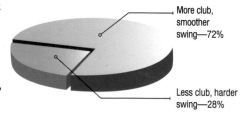

More club, smoother swing—72%

Less club, harder swing—28%

"Swinging smooth with a longer club never goes out of style, but sometimes this causes you to decelerate. Swinging a shorter club harder makes sure this never happens."
—**Top 100 Teacher Keith Lyford**

KNOCK DOWN THE PIN
Changing your setup takes yards off your shots without you having to think about it.

How to Get Precise with Your Wedges

HOW IT WORKS

Take your sand wedge and your lob wedge to the range. Hit ten balls with each club, and calculate your average distance with each. Take the difference between these two numbers and divide it by the difference in loft. For example, if your average sand wedge distance is 12 yards longer than your average lob wedge distance, and your lob wedge has four degrees more loft than your sand wedge, divide 12 by 4. This gives you the number 3, which is how many yards you subtract off the distance you hit any of your wedges when you make any of the setup changes at right. Call it your **"Distance Reduction Variable."**

EXAMPLE

Let's work with a Distance Reduction Variable of 3 yards using the example above (yours could be different, but the theory applies to any number you compute by dividing the difference in yards between your sand wedge and lob wedge by the difference in loft). If you normally hit your sand wedge 75 yards and you're 66 yards from the pin, you need to change your setup to knock 9 yards off your swing. You can do this by making any three of the setup changes at right (if you needed to subtract only 6 yards, then you'd only need to make two of the setup changes). The trick is to find the changes that feel the most comfortable to you. You may discover that you don't feel right when you choke all the way down the handle. In that case, focus on the stance-width and stance-angle changes to dial in the right distance with your hands at the top of the handle.

WHY IT WORKS

Each of the different setup changes effectively shortens your swing without you having to think about it. All you have to do is put what you feel is your best full swing on the ball, and your setup does the rest.

1 DISTANCE REDUCTION

Move your left foot back so that the toe is even with the ball of your right foot.

Narrow your stance by two clubhead widths.

Drop your grip to the middle of the handle.

2 DISTANCE REDUCTIONS

Move your left foot back so that the toe is even with the instep on your right foot.

Narrow your stance by three clubhead widths.

Drop your grip to the bottom of the handle.

3 DISTANCE REDUCTIONS

Move your left foot back so that the toe is even with the heel on your right foot.

Combining these various setup changes gives you dozens of address position options and allows you take anywhere from approximately 2 to 36 yards off each of your wedges.

Build a shotmaking arsenal that would make even a Tour pro envious by learning to vary the time your pitches stay in the air and the amount of time they spend rolling on the ground. This way, you'll have every shot covered from 40 yards and in.

5
EASY WAYS TO
PITCH
IT CLOSE

You've come up short of the green. Big deal! The Top 100's step-by-step guide to mastering pitch shots will get you to tap-in range every time.

KNOW YOUR CARRY FROM YOUR ROLL

Ask any golfer to define a pitch shot and they'll give you something that sounds very similar to a chip shot. They're partly right—a pitch shot is basically an elongated version of your chipping technique. Pitching, however, usually involves longer distances, and unlike chip shots, the quality of your pitches closely depends on your ability to produce very specific amounts of carry and roll. Some pitches require almost all carry and zero roll, while some are better suited to hitting the ground immediately and rolling all the way to the cup. Once you get the carry/roll part of the equation down pat, you'll learn to pitch with precision, and even look forward to the times when you come up short of the green on your approach.

TECHNIQUE

Your Basic Pitch

Blend the best of your full-swing and chipping moves to pitch with Tour-level precision

—Top 100 Teacher Mike Malaska

WHAT IT IS

A pitch is a less-than-full shot normally used from 10 to 50 yards of the green, and with a variety of clubs (more-lofted clubs for higher shots and more carry than roll; less-lofted clubs for lower shots and more roll than carry). Since you're not looking to hit the ball very far, your swing both back and through is much shorter—chest high is as far back as you should ever need to go. If the shot requires a longer backswing, then you're creeping outside a comfortable pitching range.

HOW TO DO IT

The most important element of your pitch swing is that everything matches up. Your arm swing—however long—should match your body turn both back and through. That makes it easy to put a good clean strike on the ball—the only true requirement of hitting a successful pitch. There are a number of different shot options when pitching (you'll learn those as you read through this chapter), but most will be a derivative of the swing you see here. Get the fundamental keys of this swing down and you'll open up your short game options like you never thought possible.

ON THE NUMBER

2:1

The ratio between the amount of carry and roll for a standard, medium-length pitch (20 to 40 yards). For example, if you're pitching the ball 30 yards, it should fly 20 yards and roll 10 yards. That's a much larger roll percentage than you're used to.

1

2

Weight favors left leg throughout.

6

7

11

Shaft and right leg angle match.

12

Arms and club following the turning action of your stomach.

BACKSWING

Everything turns away from the ball together. Instead of thinking about shoulder and hip turn when you pitch, focus on turning your stomach—doing so will tighten up your swing and give you greater control. Check out how my wrists gently cock the club up. You just need a little hinge to put some height on the shot. Also, notice how I keep a little more weight on my left side than normal. This encourages a solid downward strike on the ball.

Everything moves at the same pace—it's a connected swing.

Head holds steady— eyes on the ball.

DOWNSWING

The connection theme holds true on your downswing as well. Notice how everything is moving at the same speed, keeping pace with the turning action of my stomach. Because you hinged your wrists during your backswing, you need to gently unhinge them on the way back down. Allow your right knee to kick in a little toward the target to help transfer weight to your left foot.

"Chase" the ball with your eyes.

THROUGH-SWING

At impact, the shaft is leaning slightly toward the target and actually matches the same angle as my lower right leg. If you're prone to hitting short shots thin, pay special attention to my head—it's rock solid and focused on my strike. Once you make contact, continue to unwind at the same pace, and try to follow the ball with your eyes without lifting your head. That will help you finish your turn and guarantee solid results.

How to Pitch It Crisp From Any Lie

Changing where you play the ball in your stance gives you clean contact from the fairway, first cut or rough

—Top 100 Teacher Mike LaBauve

THIS STORY IS FOR YOU IF...

1
You always play the ball in the same spot in your stance when you pitch.

2
You don't think about how different types of grass affect your shots.

CHECK THIS!

Before attempting any pitch shot, examine your lie. In most cases your ball will be sitting up in the fairway, sitting slightly down in the first cut of rough, or submerged in sizable rough. Each of these lies requires a certain type of pitch swing to ensure the cleanest contact possible. You won't have to change your swing mechanics, just your setup so you correctly offset the effects of the grass. If you ignore your lie, the chances of getting the ball on the green won't be very good.

ON THE NUMBER

Q How close do PGA Tour pros land pitch shots?

▢ Tour average
▢ Tour leader

Data courtesy PGA Tour ShotLink

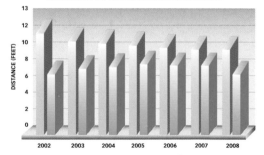

PROXIMITY TO THE HOLE FROM 20-30 YARDS

DISTANCE (FEET)

2002 2003 2004 2005 2006 2007 2008

The average PGA Tour pro pitches to 10 feet on average from 20 to 30 yards. They'll finish off the up-and-down approximately 50 percent of the time.

LIE DETECTOR
Offset the effects of long grass by playing the ball forward or back in your stance.

HOW TO ADJUST BALL POSITION FOR DIFFERENT LIES

IF THE BALL IS SITTING UP
(all of the ball sits above the grass)

Play the ball in the spot where your swing bottoms out. This gives you the cleanest possible strike since you don't have to worry about interference from the grass. If you don't know where your swing bottoms out, make a practice swing and look for the scuff mark on the grass. The center of the scuff is the bottom of your natural swing arc.

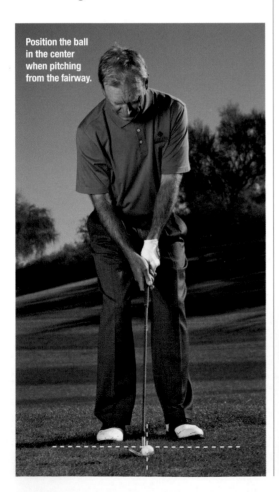

Position the ball in the center when pitching from the fairway.

IF THE BALL IS SITTING IN SLIGHT ROUGH
(3/4 of the ball sits above the grass)

Play the ball behind the spot where your swing bottoms out. Position the ball in the back of your stance (off the instep of your right foot) and set your hands in front of your zipper so that the shaft leans toward the target. This encourages ball-first, turf-second contact. If you make contact with the turf first, you won't get the distance you need to pitch the ball all the way to your target.

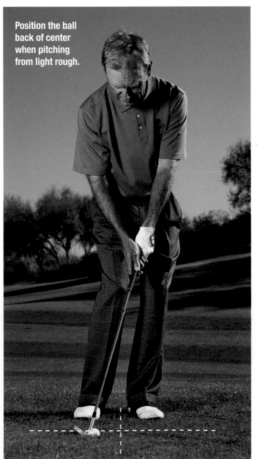

Position the ball back of center when pitching from light rough.

IF THE BALL IS IN DEEP ROUGH
(1/2 of the ball sits above the grass)

Play the ball forward of the spot where your swing bottoms out. Move the ball toward your left foot, but keep your hands in front of your zipper so that the shaft leans slightly away from the target. This puts all the loft of the club to work (the long grass has the tendency to shut down the face), and gives you the largest possible clubface area with which to make contact.

Position the ball forward of center when pitching from deep rough.

Roll & Lift to Pitch It Tight

Doing this with your right ankle on your downswing gives you the clean contact you're looking for

—Top 100 Teacher John Elliott Jr.

THIS STORY IS FOR YOU IF...

1
You often hit your pitch shots thin.

2
You never think about your footwork when you pitch.

CHECK THIS!

One way to think of your pitch swing is that it's a slightly bigger version of your chip swing—more arm swing, more wrist hinge and more body turn. The differences are pretty easy to spot, but what you might not recognize so easily is the footwork involved with both swings, which has a lot to do with how you shift your weight.

When you hit pitches and chips, you shift your weight to your left foot on your downswing, just like you do when you hit full shots from the fairway. Because your pitch swing is bigger than your chip swing (sometimes much bigger when you're pitching from long distance), you need a more pronounced shift. Focusing on your right ankle makes this happen almost automatically.

HOW TO ROLL, LIFT AND SHIFT

Once you complete your pitch backswing, allow your right ankle to roll toward the target and your heel to rise slightly off the ground. This subtle bit of downswing footwork makes it easy to shift your weight forward and contact the ball with the majority of your weight on your left foot. The next time you practice your chipping, key in on your right ankle, rolling it toward the target—then lifting your right heel—on every swing. You'll notice that it gives you the correct amount of shift and turn to catch the ball crisp. It's a good swing thought to bring to the course, and it also works for your chip swing. The only difference is that your ankle only rolls—it doesn't lift—when you're hitting a chip.

Rolling your right ankle and lifting your right heel through impact makes it easy to correctly shift your weight forward and turn through the shot.

On small chips, roll your right ankle, but don't lift it.

Grip down to the metal of the club.

Make contact just under the ball's equator.

Hover the club just above the grass.

Play a bellied wedge

You're on the fringe, but the apron is wide. You don't feel comfortable putting the ball though longer grass, but you want more precision than what you get from your everyday chip. The solution? A bellied 7-iron. Halfway between a chip and a putt, a bellied 7-iron strikes the ball with its leading edge of the club. The result is a shot that skims along the fringe before settling down to roll on the green.

Set up as you would for a putt: square stance, ball off your left heel. With your regular putting stroke, choke down to the metal of the club. Address the ball with the leading edge of the club about a quarter-inch above the ground. You want to make contact just under the ball's equator to pop up the ball enough to avoid the fringe. Use an arms-and-shoulders stroke and allow a little play in your wrists for feel.

Use an arms-and-shoulder stroke.

DRILL

Groove the Right Kind of Contact

Keeping the ball low sends your impact quality sky high

—*Top 100 Teacher Bill Davis*

THIS STORY IS FOR YOU IF...

1
Your club beats your hands to impact (i.e., fat and thin contact).

2
You've fallen in love with loft and hit every pitch too high.

THE PROBLEM

You're stuck in the bad habit of helping the ball into the air when you pitch. You think that lofting the shot skyward is the correct way to get the ball all the way to the pin.

THE SOLUTION

Your goal when pitching is to hit the ball first and the turf second. This kind of blow is critical to generating the ideal distance, loft and spin for any pitch shot.

If you're not making the right kind of contact, practice hitting low shots with your pitching wedge (thins don't count). This will get you in the good habit of hitting down on the ball, and stop your tendency to flip your hands at the bottom of your swing.

> "Trying to force loft is counter-productive to hitting a successful pitch."

HOW TO PRACTICE YOUR PITCH CONTACT

On the range, picture an imaginary bar in your mind's eye about 10 yards in front of you on your target line. Set the bar at approximately three feet off the ground, and see how many half-swing pitching wedges you can keep under it. Better yet, set dowels in the ground and form a triangle gate, and see how many pitches you can blast through the obstacle. You'll improve your contact and the quality of your pitch shots in no time.

Practicing keeping the ball low is the fast way to improve the quality of your pitch impact.

STROKE SAVER

Look for good miss spots as well as perfect plays

Regardless of how good your short game is, every green complex houses trouble spots from which making par is impossible. If you know where these trouble spots are and plan your pitch to the green so that if you do miss you won't land in them, you won't be saddled with an automatic bogey. It's the same strategy you'd use when you're looking for good miss spots from the tee box.

Three things to consider when you're trying to figure out where not to miss when pitching onto the green (these are good strategies for full-swing approaches as well):

1: SHORT-SIDED TROUBLE

If the pin is up, hit the pitch that will leave you in the center of the green. If your shot flies or rolls too far, you'll leave yourself plenty of room to chip the ball and run it up close. Pars are scarce when you're chipping with little room between you and the pin.

2: SLOPE TROUBLE

If the green slopes from back to front, err on missing short over missing long. Downhill chips and putts are more difficult to control than uphill chips and putts. (Reverse this strategy if the green slopes from front to back.)

3: HAZARD TROUBLE

Hit the club that will easily carry any trouble in front of the green, even if you mis-hit the shot. You'd rather have a long putt or chip than a tricky explosion shot from the sand.

When hitting any short approach, it's important that you accelerate through the ball. That means keeping your hands and clubhead moving through the impact area. The worst thing you can do when trying to play a pitch shot is to slow down. That's when bad things happen. Most golfers decelerate because they lack confidence—they're afraid of what they might do wrong. If you accelerate, the only thing you have to worry about is what you might do right.

How to Stop Hitting Pitches Thin

Try these drills to improve your ballstriking
and contact with short swings

—Top 100 Teacher Bill Davis

THIS STORY IS FOR YOU IF...

1
Your pitch contact feels mushy.

2
Your practice is unstructured—you don't know how to improve your pitch technique.

TRY THIS!

Set six tees in the ground so that just the caps sit above the turf. Leave about two clubhead widths between each set of tees, and place a ball on the second, fourth and sixth tees *[see photo]*. Address the first tee like you would for any standard pitch (pretend the cap of the tee is the ball), and make your swing. Try to knock the tee out of the ground. Then, move to the next tee, and use the same swing to pitch the ball crisply onto the range.

WHAT IT DOES

Knocking the tee out of the ground, then using that same swing to actually pitch a ball, gets you in the habit of hitting down, instead of hitting up and catching the shot thin. A good image to have is that you're trying to drive the target side of the ball into the grass. That's what instructors mean when they say "hit down and through." Making a downward strike like this gives you the best kind of contact for pitching (for all iron swings, really).

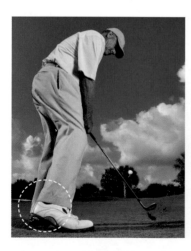

ALSO DO THIS!

Practice hitting pitches with your right heel raised slightly off the ground. This forces you to hit the ball with a majority of your weight on your left foot. This forward weight position is key to producing a downward strike, with your swing bottoming out in front of the ball, not behind it.

Alternating practice swings with real ones is a great way to groove any new skill.

DRILL

How to Tighten Up Your Pitch Swing

This tee drill helps you keep your hands ahead of the club through impact
—*Top 100 Teacher Dr. Gary Wiren*

THIS STORY IS FOR YOU IF...

1
You think a pitch swing is mostly hands and arms.

2
You never think about turning your body when you pitch.

CHECK THIS!

Stick a tee through the hole on the top of your grip, address a ball and make what you feel is a solid 50-yard pitch. Hold your finish with your hands at waist height (any higher and you will have hit the shot too far). Is the tee pointing at the left side of your torso, or is it pointing toward your stomach?

WHAT YOU'RE LOOKING AT

The relationship between your hands and your clubhead. For most short shots, you want your hands to lead the clubhead to impact. Moreover, you never want the clubhead to pass your hands as you swing into your follow-though. When this happens, your swing is too wristy and you'll hit more than your fair share of fat and thin pitches.

If the tee is pointing to the left side of your torso, then you correctly kept your hands ahead of the clubhead and used your body—not your hands—to hit the shot. If the tee is pointing at your stomach, then you flipped your hands or stopped turning your body through impact. You won't even need to look at the tee—your poor technique will show up in your results. Keep practicing this drill until you get the tee pointing at your left side every time.

Stick a tee in the hole on the top of your grip *[left]* and use it to check the quality of your swing. The tee should point to the left side of your torso in your finish. If it doesn't, then you allowed the clubhead to pass your hands.

Feel Your Way to Perfect Pitches

Think of your pitch swing as an easy underhand toss
—*Top 100 Teacher Mike LaBauve*

THIS STORY IS FOR YOU IF...

1
You have trouble controlling the distance of your pitches...

2
...as well as their height and trajectory.

PICTURE THIS!
On the range, select a nearby target—something that you can reach with a nice easy pitch. Instead of hitting a ball toward this target, toss one underhand and see how close you can get. Odds are you'll land it right on the money. That's because your eyes tell your body exactly how hard to toss the ball to cover the distance it's calculated, and you've learned to trust your eyes.

If you're having trouble controlling the distance you hit your pitch shots, start thinking of them as soft, underhand tosses. Make the same-sized motion you'd use to toss the ball to the target. The image is a useful one, not only for distance control, but also for generating the correct height and force. If you want to hit a low shot, picture a low toss; if you need to get the ball into the air, picture a high toss.

> "The more you can get away from mechanical swing thoughts, the better."

Before hitting any pitch, imagine that you're tossing a ball to the same target, then reproduce the same feeling when you hit the shot for real.

TECHNIQUE

Find the Best Ball Position for Your Swing

Move it to where the bottom of your swing occurs for precise contact
—*Top 100 Teacher Mike LaBauve*

THIS STORY IS FOR YOU IF...

1
You never think about where to play the ball in your stance on short shots.

2
You often hit pitches fat or thin.

CHECK THIS!
Before hitting any pitch, back off a few inches from the ball and make several quick practice swings, brushing your clubhead along the grass as you swing through the hitting zone. After a few brushes, look at the turf and examine the scuff mark made by the sole of your clubhead. You need to match the ball position to the scuff's position relative to your stance in order to hit consistently crisp pitches.

HOW TO POSITION THE BALL IN THE RIGHT PLACE

Ball played forward of swing bottom.

Here, my practice pitch swing left a scuff mark noticeably behind where the ball is in my stance. If I keep this forward ball position, my club will bottom out before the ball and strike it on the upswing. Thin city!

Match ball position to the scuff mark.

To adjust for the natural bottom of my swing arc, I've taken a half step to my left so that the ball is more toward the back of my stance. Notice how the ball position here matches the scuff position in the top photo relative to my stance—perfect.

TURN AROUND
Because pitch shots are short shots, golfers tend to make jabby, all-arm swings with the clubhead traveling straight back and through. That's a recipe for disaster. Think of your pitch swing as a miniature version of your full swing, including weight shift, release and, most important, a solid turn through the ball.

FEEL GRIP
Solid wedge players are usually "feel" players, which is to say that they know what the clubhead is doing at every point in their swing. One way to get this type of control is to use a lighter grip pressure when you're hitting soft pitches into the green. The moment you grip the handle too tightly is the moment your hands stop sensing what the clubhead is doing.

SEE THE SHOT

You know what one of your big drives looks like, and that's one of the reasons why you hit your driver better than your wedges. It's critical that you build an image of the type of shot you want to hit (how high it will go and what it will do when it hits the ground). Your eyes are powerful tools—they send signals to your brain that tell it how it should move. You still have to pull the trigger, but don't underestimate the power of imagination.

MASTER CLASS

Phil Mickelson

Caution: magician at work. That's the warning sign posted next to Phil Mickelson's bag whenever he's hitting a short shot into the green, although Phil rarely heeds the warning. More apt to take the high-risk-high-reward route then play the safest shot onto the green, Mickelson's game has come to define the creativity needed to save par from the most dire situations. He's not just lucky—Mickelson spends hours practicing his short-game wizardry. It's eye-popping and nothing short of amazing, yet rooted in the same fundamentals and swing principles that help even standard chips and pitches land close. Check the snapshot at left—these are the moves that help you pitch the ball with precision every time you come up short of the green.

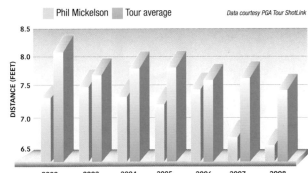

PROXIMITY TO PIN <30 YARDS (FROM FAIRWAY, ROUGH AND SAND)

Phil Mickelson ■ Tour average   *Data courtesy PGA Tour ShotLink*

When he comes up short of the green, you can count on Phil Mickelson to land his next shot extra close, sometimes up to 15 percent closer.

Plan Your Pitch Shot

These three shots take the guesswork out of pitching
—*Top 100 Teacher Mark Hackett*

THE SITUATION
You're 20 yards off the green. Your lie is good and your path is clear.

THE SMART PLAY
You're tempted to grab your sand wedge and make a long backswing if the pin is back and a short backswing if it's up. But how short is short? And how long is long? Guess wrong and you could end up miles from the hole—and that will cost you strokes. Each of the three possible pin positions (back, middle and front) requires a distinct amount of loft, spin and carry if you want to get the ball close. That means deciding whether you want the ball to sit, walk or run. Luckily, picking the right shot is a fairly easy process.

THIS STORY IS FOR YOU IF...

1 You use the same swing for every pitch shot.

2 When you try to hit high, soft shots you end up hitting grounders.

IF THE PIN IS CUT IN THE FRONT...

Closed

Square

MAKE THE BALL SIT
CLUB: Lob wedge
BALL POSITION: Forward of center.
HAND POSITION: Center.
WEIGHT: Over left foot.
Moving the ball forward in your stance increases the effective loft. This will help you add height so the ball can pop up and sit down almost immediately—the perfect recipe for when the pin is in the front.
KEY ADJUSTMENT: Whenever you play the ball forward in your stance, the clubface wants to close down and point a little left of where you're aimed. Before taking your swing, open the face a few degrees and make sure it's pointing at your target.

IF THE PIN IS CUT IN THE MIDDLE...

MAKE THE BALL HIT AND WALK

CLUB: Sand Wedge.

BALL POSITION: Center of stance.

HAND POSITION: Center (shaft straight up and down).

WEIGHT: Even.

In this situation you want to land the ball on the front third of the green and let it track to the hole. If you're more comfortable with a gap wedge, that will also work, but a sand wedge gives you a bit more spin to help slow down the roll.

KEY ADJUSTMENT: Since you've positioned the ball in the middle of your stance, both your shoulders and clubface will naturally set up square. All you need to do is make an even-paced swing both back and through.

Back Pin Position

Front Pin Position

Middle Pin Position

IF THE PIN IS CUT IN THE BACK

MAKE THE BALL HIT AND RUN

CLUB: Gap wedge.

BALL POSITION: Just inside right foot.

HAND POSITION: Center (shaft leaning slightly toward from the target).

WEIGHT: Over left foot.

Land the ball halfway between you and the pin. Since you're counting on the ball rolling just as far as it flies in the air, make sure you know which way it will break once it hits the turf.

KEY ADJUSTMENT: Whenever you play the ball back in your stance, the clubface wants to open up and point a little right of where you're aimed. Rotate the face a few degrees to get it pointing at your target.

Open

Square

SHOTMAKING

Bump It On and Close

This part-carry, part-roll beauty is a bona fide par-saver when you come up short of the green

—*Top 100 Teacher Carol Presinger*

THIS STORY IS FOR YOU IF...

1
You're coming up short on long par 4s and par 5s...

2
...and you can't get the ball close enough on your third shot to save par.

THE SITUATION
You're in no-man's land—40 yards from the green with a tight lie. You're finding yourself in this position more often than in the past as courses get longer and longer.

THE SMART PLAY
Despite advances in technology in every facet of the game over the last two decades, the best play for when you come up short of the green is one that's been around for a hundred years: the bump-and-run pitch. It's one of the easiest shots you can hit, as long as you follow a few simple rules and convince yourself that landing the ball short of the pin is the best way to get it close. Here's how to do it.

TOP 100 TEACHER POLL

Q Should you use mostly carry or mostly roll to get pitch shots close?

Roll it close—88%

Fly it close—12%

"Everything depends on the situation. If there's a hazard in the way, then of course you need to use more carry than roll. As a general rule, however, the more you can keep the ball on the ground, the better."
—Top 100 Teacher Brady Riggs

STEP 1 SELECT A LANDING AREA

For a bump and run, a good rule of thumb is to fly the ball two-thirds of the way and let it run along the ground toward the hole the final one-third. If the pin is up, that means landing the ball short of the green, which is perfectly okay for this situation. When you pick your spot, imagine a lower trajectory, not a high-arcing balloon shot. This will put you in the proper state of mind when selecting your target.

HOW TO SAVE PAR WHEN YOUR APPROACH LANDS SHORT

STEP 2 SET UP FOR A SOFT, LOW SHOT

Take a narrow stance with your left foot slightly open to your target. This will help you turn through the shot—something amateurs forget to do on short swings. Play the ball back of center, and set your hands off the inside of your left thigh. Notice how the shaft leans toward the target when you do this. You'll want to re-create this same lean at impact.

STEP 3 MAKE A SHORT BACKSWING

With a 9-iron, all you need to do is take your hands back to waist height with just a touch of wrist hinge. This will give you about 25 yards of carry and 15 yards of roll. (If you need to hit it farther, use an 8-iron. For shorter shots, drop to a pitching wedge.) Notice how my lower body is calm and relaxed. Start sliding here and you'll have trouble making crisp contact.

STEP 4 TURN AND RELEASE

Your backswing length controls the distance of the shot, so there's no need to adjust your through-swing to manipulate the ball close. Turn through like you do on normal full swings, stopping your hands, again, at waist height. It's important that you release the club through impact so that you strike the ball with a square clubface. You'll know you did it right if the toe of your iron points toward the sky in your finish.

How to Hit a Super-High Pitch

It's easy to do when you activate your wrists

—*Top 100 Teacher Bill Forrest*

THIS STORY IS FOR YOU IF...

1
You know that some shots require more carry than roll...

2
...but you're not sure how to get the ball high in the air.

THE SITUATION

You're within easy pitch range of the flag (about 30 yards), but there's a hazard fronting the green, and there's not much room between the hazard and the flagstick.

THE SOLUTION

There's only one: an extra-high pitch. This short-flying, high-floating gem is an asset to any player's short game, even from tight lies in the fairway (where a lot of recreational players tend to thin the shot when attempting to produce extra height). Unlike flops and other short-game tricks, a super-high pitch requires that you make your usual pitch swing, but add in a lot more wrist hinge. The secret is to hinge your wrists early and fully in your backswing, then do the same as you swing into your follow-through. That extra hinge—especially as you release it through impact—is vital to getting the ball to fly high and directly at your target.

HIGH FLYER
A little bit of extra hand action at the bottom of your swing adds extra loft to the clubface, and gives the shot extra height and stopping power.

THE HIGH-PITCH BACKSWING

A

Ball forward, shaft straight up and down.

B

Make an early and full wrist hinge.

C

Hinge gives you height-producing power.

HOW TO PITCH IT EXTRA HIGH TO A TUCKED PIN

Swing back down like normally, leading the clubhead with your hands. An early release destroys any chance of getting the ball high into air.

As you feel your clubhead enter the impact zone, begin to unload the hinge in your wrists. This unhinging action adds extra loft to your clubface.

At impact, you want to feel like the clubhead is directly underneath your hands as you continue to unfold the angle of your wrists.

The extra loft at impact pops the ball almost straight up. But don't quit now—continue to unhinge your wrists as you swing into your follow-through.

Although your wrist hinge is essential to this shot, so is speed. Make your normal-paced swing, turning through the shot like you would on any long pitch.

Continue unhinging your wrists. If you do it correctly, the toe of your wedge will point at the sky by the time your hands reach hip height in your forward-swing.

Get A Feel For High Pitches

This pre-swing practice drill gets you in the groove for extra loft

—*Top 100 Teacher Scott Munroe*

THIS STORY IS FOR YOU IF...

1
You get nervous when attempting high pitches.

2
You need a pre-swing thought to give you more confidence.

TRY THIS!
The next time you need to pull off a high pitch shot, step away from the ball and hold your wedge out in front of you with only your left hand on the handle (like you're resting on a cane). Make a mock backswing with your right hand only, and then a mock through-swing. Your goal is to swing your right arm through the gate created by the shaft and your left arm.

As you perform this drill, you'll notice that you need to add some hip and shoulder turn in order to swing all the way through the gate. Perfect—you'll need that when you go to hit the shot for real. More important, focus on keeping your right palm facing the target through impact, and then pointing it skyward as you swing through the gate. This right-palm up position is the secret to hitting high-lofted pitches, especially from tight lies.

Perform the drill a few times in succession, then hit your shot. The feeling you grooved in the drill will pay off in a perfect high pitch that lands soft and trickles to a stop.

Keep your right palm facing the sky to practice pitching the ball with extra height.

Simple, easy right-arm only swings make your pitch motion smoother after only a few attempts.

DRILL

How to Pitch It Smooth

Hit balls one-handed to smoothen out your pitch mechanics

—*Top 100 Teacher Bill Forrest*

THIS STORY IS FOR YOU IF...

1
You're normally a fast swinger.

2
You tend to rush your pitch shots.

DO THIS!

When you're at the end of a practice bucket, or even when you're standing on the tee box waiting for the group in front of you to clear the fairway, hit some practice pitches with your sand wedge using only your right arm. Don't try to kill the ball—just make a smooth backswing and even smoother follow-through, like you're trying to hit the ball 20 yards. Swinging with only your right arm frees up your motion since you have less control of the clubhead, and it forces you to accelerate through impact while turning toward the target (if you don't your right wrist will flip and you'll hit a grounder). You'll know you're doing it right when your wrist doesn't flip and you catch the ball clean while finishing your swing with the club looking like a natural extension of your right arm.

If you can get good at pitching balls with only your right arm, you'll be an expert when you hit them on the course with both hands on the handle. You can even do this drill without a ball. It's excellent for building the proper motion and, even more important, the correct speed and tempo (try to do this one fast and you'll never get it right).

Hit It Soft & Short

Change your setup to handle delicate pitches using your everyday motion

—Top 100 Teacher Kellie Stenzel

THE SITUATION

You missed on your approach and are sitting a few yards off the green. You're thinking putter, but the grass is too long to roll the ball safely onto the putting surface.

THE SMART PLAY

There's only one: an extra-small pitch. Successfully hitting this shot isn't a matter of force like most golfers believe, but rather a matter of swing length. Make the following setup changes to limit how far you take the club back, so you can hit the ball just enough to land on the green using your everyday motion.

CHOKE UP
Set your hands near the bottom of the grip so that your right thumb is nearly touching the shaft. This makes your sand wedge or lob wedge much shorter and automatically reduces the amount of power you can deliver to the ball.

THIS STORY IS FOR YOU IF...

1
You'd rather putt from off the green than hit a small pitch because you always catch these shots thin.

2
You think short shots require a slow swing.

NARROW YOUR STANCE
Set up with the ball in the middle of your stance and your feet almost touching. This ultra-narrow stance limits the flexibility in your hips, so you turn less and cut your backswing way short without having to think about it.

MAKE A THUMP
Your choke grip and narrow stance make it easy to stop the club short using your normal tempo. Come back into the ball with a smooth acceleration, and "thump" the ground under the ball with the sole of your wedge. The ball will come off the face softly and cleanly and fly the short distance you need.

TECHNIQUE

TECHNIQUE

Flop It High and Soft

Try this "fingers off" trick to pop short shots almost straight up in the air

—Top 100 Teacher Martin Hall

THE SITUATION

You're near the green, but the pin is tucked behind a hazard, or it's set hard near the front edge of a green surrounded by rough. You need loft, and lots of it.

THE SOLUTION

You need to flop this ball high and soft—not always an easy assignment when the ball is sitting on a tight fairway lie. Whereas on most shots you want to avoid scooping the ball into the air, here's where a little scoop can do a bit—check that, a lot—of good. The following tip is an easy way to introduce some scoop—and loft—into your swing.

HOW TO LOFT IT EXTRA-HIGH

As you feel your club enter the impact zone, lift the last three fingers on your left hand off the grip. Removing these fingers allows your clubhead to slide underneath the ball instead of driving into the back of it. This slipping action adds extra loft to your clubface, helping to launch the ball extra high. Players like Greg Norman and Seve Ballesteros used this trick from time to time to scoop the ball up and reach tough pins they couldn't get to with a standard pitch.

THIS STORY IS FOR YOU IF...

1
Your game is in need of a lob shot.

2
A lob shot? Isn't that for Tour players only?

THE *GM* VAULT

Teach Yourself Touch
PGA Tour player
Greg Norman
GOLF Magazine, June 1985

How to nip the ball from a tight lie

Here, the bounce on your sand wedge works against you. Opt for your 8-iron, play the ball in the middle of your stance and take the club back to the inside. Then, pull the club down with your hands, and roll your right hand over your left through impact. This nip shot is good for carrying obstacles and letting the ball run out.

> "Don't let tight lies fool you. Short grass means you have to make absolutely perfect contact."

Hit the One-Hop-and-Stop Pitch

This shot lands close then bites harder than a miner's handshake
—*Top 100 Teacher Jim Murphy*

WHAT IT IS

A crisp pitch shot that hits the green, takes one hop forward and then stops because it's spinning faster than a top on steroids.

WHEN TO USE IT

From a good lie in the fairway when you have about 30 yards to the green. The pin is cut in the front—if you hit a normal pitch the ball will hit the green and run past the hole. You need this thing to land and then stop.

HOW TO HIT IT

To stop the ball like you want you'll need clubhead speed and a trapping type of impact, where the club literally pinches the ball against the turf. Most amateur players have difficulty trapping the ball on full swings. The trick is to take a stance that makes it happen automatically. Follow the steps below.

THIS STORY IS FOR YOU IF...

1 Your pitches tend to roll out more than you'd like.

2 You've always admired the way pros make their short approaches stop on a dime.

TRAP ACTION
You get extra spin when you trap the ball against the turf at impact. "Scoopy" impact gives you a knuckle ball.

WEIGHT LEFT
Set up with your right foot raised on its toe. This will help you keep your weight forward so you can properly hit down on the ball.

HOW TO STOP THE BALL ON A DIME

STEP 1
Grab your sand wedge and open the face a few degrees—you're going to swing fast here so you need extra loft or the ball will carry too far.

Open the face just a few degrees.

STEP 2
Play the ball off your left foot and shift all of your weight forward. This makes it easier to trap the ball against the turf. To make sure your weight stays forward, set your right foot on its big toe. From here, make a hip-high backswing and keep your weight over your left leg.

Lift your right foot to set your weight.

STEP 3
On your downswing, move the club with your body as well as your hands—like your whole left side is pulling the club down and into the back of the ball. This is not a shot you're trying to pick clean. Accelerate through the ball and dig up some turf.

LANDING PAD
The ball should travel on a slight arc—if you hit a lobber, you didn't trap the ball and you won't get the spin you need. Since the ball is going to stop once it hits, pick an aggressive landing spot and leave yourself an easy chance at birdie.

STEP 4
Keep accelerating through impact and swing left of the target on your follow-through. Since all you're trying to do is trap the ball, cut your finish when your hands reach about hip height. You'll know you did it right if your clubhead and chest point left of the target.

Finish left of the target.

STROKE SAVER

Alter clubface position in your backswing to change the height of your pitches

THE SITUATION
Your approach landed short of the green, and you're sitting too far away from the pin to chip the bal. There's no room for errors in accuracy or distance control on these tricky half-wedges.

THE SOLUTION
Cut your troubles in half by changing the height of your shot to match your lie. Creating the correct trajectory takes the guesswork out of determining how to get this ball close. If you can dial your half-wedges high or low depending on the situation, you'll have an excellent chance of getting up and down from anywhere.

HIT A HIGH-TRAJECTORY PITCH SHOT
When you have to carry a bunker or don't have much green to work with.

● High shots eliminate any trouble between you and your target.

● On your backswing, cup your left wrist (bend it back), which will open the clubface and add loft to the shot.

● You'll know you're doing it right if you look down and can see the logo on the back of your glove.

HIT A LOW-TRAJECTORY PITCH SHOT
When the front of the green is open or when there's plenty of room between the apron and the pin.

● Hitting it low and letting the ball run means you don't have to hit the ball a perfect distance in the air.

● Bend your left wrist forward on your takeaway. This bowing action closes the clubface and takes loft off the club.

● If you look down at your hands and can't see the logo on your glove, you're doing this right.

The most important asset when chipping is confidence. Without it you'll make cautious, decelerating strokes that won't get the ball close enough for a save. Confidence comes with practice—the Top 100 teachers are here to show you the way.

6

CAN'T MISS CHIP SHOTS

Short shots around the green are long on importance. Here's how to approach each one with confidence and land it close to the hole

SAVE PAR LIKE A TOUR PRO

It's very rare for a skilled golfer to miss wildly from around the green. After all, these are short shots made with even shorter swings with the target in clear view. If a Tour pro fails to get the ball close from around the green, then he experienced a major malfunction that won't likely be repeated soon. Amateurs, on the other hand, miss short shots all the time. It's a confidence issue—you don't trust your technique, so you end up making a cautious stroke that more often than not puts you in a tough putting situation—or on the other side of the green. In this chapter, you'll learn how to perfect your chip technique using several drills, so that when it comes time to chip on the course, you'll do it almost automatically. That's when you start to consistently get the ball close and earn more than your fair share of up-and-downs.

Your Basic Chip

Learning the right moves keeps your scores in the red and your enjoyment sky high

—Top 100 Teacher Kellie Stenzel

THIS STORY IS FOR YOU IF...

1
You often hit your chips fat or thin.

2
Your chips fly too far or too short of your target.

3
Your chipping impact sounds like a "thud" instead of a "click."

WHAT IT IS

A chip shot is a short shot hit with a variety of clubs, but most often with your sand, gap and lob wedges. It's a tiny stroke—more like a putting stroke than what you use for a pitch or full swing. In fact, many players hit the shot like it's a putt, but with a wedge and with a wedge setup.

HOW TO HIT IT

The secret is to put a controlled strike on the ball without decelerating, which is something most amateurs struggle with. Since the shot is so short, the tendency is to slow down into impact. The key is to keep everything moving, especially at impact.

Some good advice: make sure you keep your left arm moving toward the target all the way through the shot. Your left arm is the motor of your chip, and if you use it correctly it will swing past your left leg in your forward-stroke. You can check to see if you're doing this by hitting practice chips and simply holding your finish position.

TURN THE PAGE TO LEARN HOW TO CHIP IT CLOSE EVERY TIME

TOP 100 TEACHER POLL

Q Should I chip like it's a putt or use a small pitch swing?

→ Putting stroke—69%

→ Pitch swing—31%

"Hitting a chip like it's a putt removes the need to swing on an arc, minimizing the chance that you'll hit the ball off line."
—Top 100 Teacher Mike Perpich

To avoid deceleration, make sure your left arm finishes in front of your left leg without the clubhead flipping past your hands.

1

Weight forward, ball back of center, shaft leaning toward target.

2

3

Club powered by the triangle formed by your shoulders and arms.

7

Left arm continually moves toward the target on your through-swing.

8

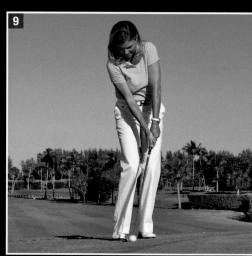

9

How to Hit A Chip Shot

Copy the positions here to stop the ball close on every chip

—*Top 100 Teacher Kellie Stenzel*

STOP ERRORS AT THE START

As with most shots, you can eliminate the majority of errors if you make sure your setup is correct. The goal of your chipping address position is to situate your body, arms, hands and club to create a descending blow without chunking the clubhead into the ground, or striking the ball with the leading edge of the clubface.

Stand far enough away from the ball so that you can bend forward from your hips and get your

4 Add a touch of wrist hinge to enhance feel.

5

6

10 Left wrist perfectly flat at the point of impact.

11

12 Left arm stays straight and moves past your left leg.

chest over your toes. Do it correctly and you'll feel like your arms are hanging straight down without touching your torso or your legs. Set the majority of your weight over your left foot, and try to keep it there during your stroke. If your weight moves to your right foot, you'll likely catch the chip thin.

SWING THE TRIANGLE

Think of your chip swing as an elongated version of your putting stroke. Swing the club back using the triangle formed by your shoulders and arms. A bit of wrist hinge is okay to add some feel to the shot, but as you strike the ball you want your left wrist to be as flat as possible. Keep the triangle—and specifically, your left arm—moving all the way through the shot. Stopping movement leads to deceleration and a poor result. If you copy the positions above, you'll get the majority of your chips into tap-in range and save par more often than not.

> "Keep your left arm moving toward the target so it finishes ahead of your left leg."

TECHNIQUE

How to Finish Your Chip Swing

Ending your motion the right way almost guarantees a solid result

—*Top 100 Teacher Tim Mahoney*

THIS STORY IS FOR YOU IF...
1 You don't know how to control the distance of your chips.
2 You never think about the forward side of your chip swing.

THE PROBLEM

You haven't hit a solid chip in two years. You're not catching the ball in the sweet spot, and when you do you have absolutely zero control of distance.

THE SOLUTION

Here's a little-known fact about the chip swing that will likely cure your short-game problems for good: your hands and the clubhead should never get higher than your waist in your follow-through. Make a few chip swings and try to mimic the positions in the photo at right. When you take this new move to the course, you'll hit the crisp chips your game has been missing.

ON THE NUMBER

Q How close do PGA Tour pros land chips from around the green?

■ Tour average
■ Tour leader

Data courtesy PGA Tour ShotLink

PROXIMITY TO THE HOLE FROM THE FRINGE

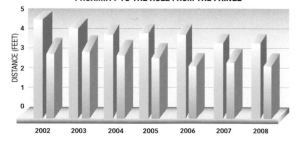

DISTANCE (FEET) — 0 1 2 3 4 5

2002 2003 2004 2005 2006 2007 2008

When Tour players miss greens, they almost always make up for their mistakes by getting their chip shots ultra-close. That's a big reason why they post such low numbers.

NO!
Bad things happen when you try to help the ball into the air. Swinging low-to-high like this in your follow-through produces skulls, fat contact and poor distance control.

YES!
Try to maintain the hand and arm positions you established at address. Turn all the way through the ball and trust the loft built into your club to get the ball up.

AVOID THE BEND
Think of the shaft as an extension of your left arm.

How to Avoid Fat Contact

Set your left wrist angle at address so that you always catch it clean

—*Top 100 Teacher Mike Adams*

THIS STORY IS FOR YOU IF...

1
You use your normal full-swing setup when chipping.

2
You tend to take too much dirt when you chip.

DO THIS!

Take your normal chipping address position and look at your left wrist. If you can see wrinkles in the fold of your wrist, then you've created too much of an angle between the shaft and your arms. This is perfectly fine when you're swinging the club full because it sets your swing plane up on an arc, but when chipping, you want your motion to be as linear (i.e., straight-back-and-through) as possible.

THEN DO THIS!

When you set up, stand close enough to the ball so that you remove the up-and-down fold in your left wrist. You shouldn't see any wrinkles below the base of your left thumb. This sets your club on a more upright lie and encourages a more back-and-through motion. This is the easiest path to strike the ball without taking too much dirt. As soon as you start making more of a circular motion, the likelihood of digging into the ground increases.

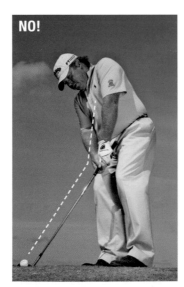

NO!

With your normal full-swing setup, the club is angled to swing on an arc, increasing the chance of hitting short shots fat.

YES!
Stand closer to the ball to straighten your left wrist and set the shaft on a more vertical angle. A more upright shaft makes it easy to swing the club straight back and through.

The Key to Crisp Contact

The secret's in your legs, not your hands and arms

—*Top 100 Teacher John Elliott Jr.*

THIS STORY IS FOR YOU IF...

1
Your chips feel like chops.

2
You don't make consistent contact, and therefore have trouble controlling the distance you hit your chips.

THE PROBLEM

You aren't putting a solid strike on the ball when you chip, even though you try to make as controlled as swing as possible and keep everything quiet.

THE SOLUTION

Sure, it's a small swing, but your chip motion needs some of the elements that make your full swing work, too. One of the most overlooked is leg action—most golfers assume that you need to keep your legs extra-quiet when you chip. True, you can't move them like you do when swinging a driver, but a little leg action goes a long way toward helping you produce the right kind of contact when you chip.

HOW TO MAKE THE RIGHT KIND OF CHIP STRIKE

On your way back to the ball, allow your right leg to kink—it should feel like your right knee is gently moving toward the target as you swing through the impact zone. Notice *[large photo, right]* how this angles my lower right leg, and how this angle matches the lean of the shaft as the clubhead approaches the ball. The two go hand-in-hand, and they're what allow you to hit slightly down on the ball and get the type of crisp contact you're looking for.

MATCH GAME
Kink your left knee so that the angle in your lower right leg matches the angle of the shaft as it approaches impact.

When your legs stay still or fail to move toward the target, you'll have difficulty creating the correct angle of attack.

TECHNIQUE

How to Chip It Straight

Use your knuckles to square the clubface and chip the ball exactly where you're aimed
—*Top 100 Teacher Anne Cain*

CHECK THIS!

Make your normal chip swing and stop. Look at the knuckles on your left hand. If you're like most golfers, they're probably pointing toward the sky. This means your clubface is open (unless you use an ultra-strong chipping grip), which is why your chips often dribble out to the right.

As you swing through impact, you want your left-hand knuckles to point toward the ground. This means your clubface is square, allowing you to contact the ball with the sweet spot of your wedge and, more important, with the leading edge pointing at your target.

Think of it as a gentle rolling of your left hand so that, at the very least, your knuckles don't point at the sky. If you overdo it, you'll start pulling your chips to the left.

KNUCKLE DOWN
Point your left-hand knuckles toward the ground through impact to square up the face.

THIS STORY IS FOR YOU IF...

1
Most of your chips dribble off to the right.

2
You've been known to shank a chip or two.

TRY THIS!

Use a strong grip for crisp chips

Putting and chipping go hand-in-hand—good chipping can leave you with easier putts, and you can salvage a bad chipping day by rolling the ball well. But if your chipping game is leaving you with long putts on just about every hole, and you can't seem to make solid contact on those delicate short shots around the green, you may want to take a look at your grip. If you've been using a standard neutral grip, with both thumbs on top of the shaft, you may benefit from taking a stronger hand position on the club. To do this, turn both hands slightly to the right and hold on firmly with your left hand. Keep your wrists firm, your hands ahead of the clubface and the back of your left hand facing the target through impact. Hit slightly down on the ball without allowing your right hand to roll over your left, and keep the clubhead moving down the line after impact. You'll have more control over the clubhead, and the ball should jump off the clubface and down your intended line.

Keep your wrists firm and keep the back of your left hand moving down the target line.

Turn both hands slightly to the right and hold on firmly with your left hand.

Hit slightly down on the ball. Your right hand shouldn't roll over your left.

Keep the clubhead moving down the line.

How to Hit a High, Soft Chip

Keep the face open to get it close when you've short-sided your approach shot
—*Top 100 Teacher Bill Forrest*

THIS STORY IS FOR YOU IF...

1
You can't handle short chips.

2
You tend to blade the ball on short swings.

THE PROBLEM
You can't stop chip shots close to the hole when there's little room between you and the pin.

WHY IT'S HAPPENING
You're not making full use of the loft built into the face of your wedge. In fact, you're probably taking loft *off* the club, which is why these shots run past the hole when you hit them. Or, in an attempt to force the ball into the air, you flip your hands at impact and catch the shot thin. Not only does this one run past the flag, it runs to the other side of the green.

THE SOLUTION
When you need to chip it short, high and soft, keep the face of your wedge from closing down at impact. In your release, the face of your wedge should look flat as a pancake [*photo, right*]. When you keep the face open like this, you have the best chance of hitting the high shot you need when there's little room between you and the pin.

NO!
Releasing the club is good on full swings but not when you're facing a delicate chip.

YES!
Keep the face open in your release to add height to your chip shots.

KEEP IT OPEN
Hold off your normal release to unlock the lofting power of your clubface.

DRILL

Chip It All the Way to the Hole

This easy drill teaches you to accelerate so you don't come up short

—*Top 100 Teacher Martin Hall*

THIS STORY IS FOR YOU IF...

1
You tend to decelerate when chipping...

2
...because most of your chips end up short of the hole.

TRY THIS!

Stick a shaft or dowel in the green at a 45-degree angle a foot outside your left toe with the grip pointing away from you *[see photo, below]*. Set up for a normal chip, then make your best move. The goal of this drill is to make clean contact without swinging past the shaft. You might have difficulty at first—if you're like most golfers you tend to decelerate on the way to the ball, then speed up after impact once you feel you haven't given the shot enough force. (Or you swing too fast from the get-go and make too long of a forward swing. In this case, you're running chips way past the hole.) Focus on accelerating to the ball and giving it a nice pop without swinging past the shaft. Once you groove this kind of motion, you'll find most of your chips covering the distance you planned, and the quality of your contact will skyrocket.

POP, THEN STOP
Hit chips with enough force to land them near your target, but don't swing past the shaft. This drill teaches you how to accelerate so you never come up short.

How to Stop Thinning Chips

Get your left eye closer to the ground at setup

—*Top 100 Teacher Martin Hall*

THIS STORY IS FOR YOU IF...

1
You tend to blade chips across the green.

2
You lack confidence when chipping.

THE PROBLEM

If you're like most golfers, you set up with your right shoulder closer to the ground than your left one, and also with your head tilted so that your right eye is closer to the ground than your left eye *[photo, below]*. While this kind of setup works with longer clubs (and especially with your driver), it's bad news for chipping. It causes your swing to bottom out too early. Your club hits the ground, bounces off the turf and strikes the equator of the ball, giving you a thinner.

THE SWING THOUGHT THAT FIXES IT

As you settle into your address position, feel like your left eye is closer to the ground than your right one *[photo, right]*.

Get into your address position and cock your head to the left, so that your left eye is closer to the ground than your right. Notice how this levels your shoulders and helps distribute your weight evenly over your feet. Now the bottom of your swing arc is underneath the ball—where it needs to be for solid chip contact. This reduces the likelihood that you'll hit behind the ball and thin it across the green.

NO!

Setting up with your right eye closer to the ground than your left is good for full swings, but not for chips.

YES!
Get your left eye closer to the ground than your right to stop your tendency to hit chips thin.

NEW METHODS

How to Be Consistent

Try chipping left-hand low for a smoother motion

—*Top 100 Teacher Kellie Stenzel*

THIS STORY IS FOR YOU IF...

1
You have zero distance control.

2
You have zero swing control.

THE PROBLEM

You're knocking chips all over the place because you have difficulty controlling the length of your chipping backstroke.

THE SOLUTION

Chip with a left-hand-low grip. Placing your left hand lower on the handle makes it harder to swing your arms and hands away from the target. It's the same reason why golfers who struggle with controlling the length of their putting stroke use a left-hand-low putting grip. Make everything the same, but grip your wedge left-hand low and make your stroke. You'll instantly feel how this grip automatically cuts the length of your backswing, which should give you the confidence to swing forward with acceleration and momentum into a solid follow-through. Try the left-hand-low grip in practice. You'll find that it's so effective—especially on short chips— that you'll bring it out to the course.

> "You can't control your chips without first controlling your backswing length."

LEFT-HAND LOW
The popular putting grip can also save your chip swing.

STROKE SAVER

Use your chips to sink more putts

When you're planning your short approaches (or even your long ones), don't always go for the pin. Often, the best place to land your ball is away from the hole, but on a specific section of the green. Why? Some putts are easier than others.

Uphill putts are easier than downhill putts (so it's a good idea to leave your chips below the hole). **Right-to-left putts are easier than straight ones,** and both of these are easier than a left-to-right putt (so it's a good idea to leave your chips on the right side of the pin if the green slopes back to front and the left side of the pin if the green slopes front to back). Straight putts have to be hit perfectly to go in (you have more margin for error when the putt breaks).

The worst combination is downhill and left-to-right— Human beings don't make those. Every golfer wants to leave the shortest putt possible, or even hole out when playing a shot from around the green. However, aggressive plays almost always leave a longer putt when they backfire.

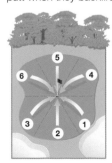

Putt difficulty
(1=easiest, 6=hardest)

CHIP GEOMETRY

Check out the triangle formed by Els' shoulders, arms and hands. He establishes this triangle intact, then swings it back and through without changing its shape. This makes your chipping stroke more like a putting stroke. Copy this straight-back-and-through motion for consistent contact and directional control.

FORWARD MOTION

Notice how Els remains in complete control of the clubhead after impact. He continues to move his arms toward the target with his hands ahead of the clubhead. This is the spot where amateurs tend to quit on the shot for fear they've made too big a swing. That's the fast-track to catching the chip fat or thin.

BRUSH IMPACT

If you're guilty of taking a divot when you chip, or don't contact the grass at all, then make practice swings, brushing the grass with your clubhead both back and through. You want to achieve the type of impact you see here—the club nips the ball off the turf while gliding across the blades. A big reason Els and other top chippers can do this is that they stay in their address posture from start to finish.

Ernie Els

Y ou'd think that a power player like Ernie Els wouldn't have to rely on a deft short game to remain competitive on Tour. His length off the tee allows him to hit shorter irons into greens than his competitors. Although short- and mid-irons are easy to control and get close, even the most skilled golfers miss with them from time to time, making a top-notch chipping game not only a luxury, but a necessity. Ernie knows this, and, surprisingly, has one of the best short-game touches the game has seen from a big man. In six of the last seven seasons, Els has topped the Tour average in scrambling from the fringe. He led the Tour in that statistical category in 2002, the year he bagged his first British Open and third major championship.

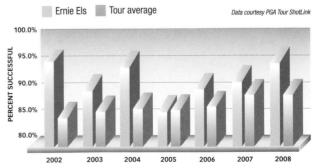

SCRAMBLING FROM THE FRINGE

◼ Ernie Els ◼ Tour average   *Data courtesy PGA Tour ShotLink*

Els has beat the Tour average in Scrambling in six of the last seven seasons.

SWING THOUGHT

Smooth Out Your Chip Shots

Add a little leg action for maximum feel and control
—Top 100 Teacher Don Kotnik

For smoother chips, take the club back like normal...

...then push your right knee toward the target.

THIS STORY IS FOR YOU IF...

1
You don't feel comfortable over short shots.

2
Your chip swing is mostly arms and hands.

TRY THIS!

The next time you practice your chip stroke, make everything the same—same setup, same grip, same ball position and same backswing—but on the way back down, add a touch of lower-body action by pushing your right knee toward the target as you swing though impact. It should feel like your legs are leaning in the direction the ball is headed.

WHAT IT DOES

This extra bit of lower-body action makes your overall move much smoother, and eliminates the chance that you'll flip your hands at the bottom of the stroke and skull the ball. Plus, when you lean your lower body toward the target on your downswing, you lead the club with your hands and get that nice pop on the ball, lofting it gently into the air without trying to lift it or help it off the ground. With practice, you'll find this move easy to make, whether the chip is short or long, giving you the confidence you need to get up and down from anywhere around the green.

DRILL

How to Gain Chipping Touch

This easy drill helps you dial in the right distance every time
—*Top 100 Teacher Laird Small*

THIS STORY IS FOR YOU IF...

1
You don't get up and down very often.

2
You wish you could control the speed of your chips better.

TRY THIS!

Practice chipping while looking at the target, not the ball. When you focus on the target, you're more apt to turn your body toward the target in your follow-through—an absolute must. Once you get used to it, your club will bottom out at the same place every time, giving you great touch and control.

On the course, take your practice swings while looking at the hole, making sure to brush the grass with your clubhead. This will help you feel how your body and club move together, and you'll be more confident on your short-game shots.

ON THE NUMBER

Q What's a good percentage to get up and down from around the green?

☐ Tour average
☐ Tour leader

Data courtesy PGA Tour ShotLink

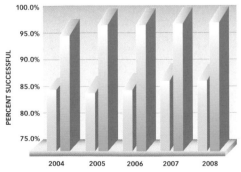

SCRAMBLING FROM THE FRINGE

PERCENT SUCCESSFUL

100.0%
95.0%
90.0%
85.0%
80.0%
75.0%

2004   2005   2006   2007   2008

Take a look at the gaudy scrambling numbers from the PGA Tour. The best players get up and down almost every time they hit a chip from the fringe.

EYE ON THE PRIZE
Looking at the hole gives you more control over your chips.

How to Chip It High or Low

Your thumbs hold the key
—Top 100 Teacher Carol Presinger

THIS STORY IS FOR YOU IF...

1
You can't control the trajectory of your chips.

2
You almost always chip the ball too low.

THE SITUATION
You're in easy chipping distance of the hole, but torn between hitting a low chip and letting it run out to the hole, or hitting it higher so it lands soft and rolls just a few inches. There will be times when you'll have the option to play either type of shot, and there will be others when the situation forces you to chip the ball high or low. It's good to know how to do both just in case.

THE SMART PLAY
Take your normal grip, and notice how your thumbs point down toward the ground when you settle into your stance. Those big digits of yours are the secret to chipping the ball lower or higher. As a general rule, the more your keep your thumbs pointing toward the ground in your swing, the lower you'll hit the chip, and the more you start pointing them to the sky in your swing, the higher you'll hit the chip.

Point your thumbs toward the ground.

HOW TO HIT A LOW CHIP
Focus on keeping your thumbs pointing toward the ground during your backswing *[above]*. That means keeping your wrists from hinging. The club should feel like an extension of your left arm when you complete your backswing. Make everything else in your swing the same.

Your thumbs-down backswing and thumbs-down impact *[right]* create a very shallow swing arc, so the ball can't run up the face and launch high off the club. You get a nice low trajectory that's easy to control—just change the length of your backswing to dial in the right distance.

USE IT...
● When you don't have to carry an obstacle.
● The pin is on an elevated tier.
● There's little room between you and the pin.
● Ultra-tight lies.

Point your thumbs toward the sky.

HOW TO HIT A HIGH CHIP

Keep everything the same, but this time try to get your thumbs to point toward the sky in your backswing *[above]*. Notice that as you point your thumbs up, your wrists hinge, setting the clubhead above your hands.

Your thumbs-up backswing and thumbs-down impact *[right]* create a very steep swing arc. At contact, the ball runs up the face and launches higher than the loft built into your clubhead. You get a nice high trajectory, a soft landing and little roll. Dial in the right distance by the length of your backswing, not by speeding up or slowing down your swing.

USE IT...

● When you're forced to carry an obstacle.
● The pin is on a lower tier.
● There's ample room between you and the pin.
● Fluffy lies.

FROM THE *GM* VAULT

Hit The No-Risk Chip
By PGA Tour player Hubert Green
GOLF Magazine, July 1977

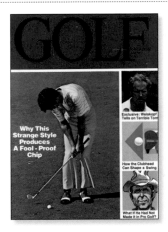

"Funny" is the word used most often to describe my chip technique. I play the ball outside my right foot and grip all the way down to the metal below the shaft. I then make a wristy stroke—my arms barely move at all. Only after impact do I let my arms and shoulders get into the act, as I extend the club outward toward the target. I'll use this technique with anything from SW to 4-iron, allowing me to chip the ball from 10 to 100 feet.

"A way-back ball position and wristy stroke gives chips a very low trajectory, which will help you keep them on line."
—Hubert Green

Claw Your Way to Crisper Chips

This unique grip helps you keep your left arm moving forward through the shot
—*Top 100 Teacher Kellie Stenzel*

THIS STORY IS FOR YOU IF...

1
You follow a good chip with a bad one on the next hole.

2
You never think about your left arm when chipping.

TRY THIS!

Take your grip in the middle of the handle, but instead of placing your right hand below your left, simply wrap it around your left hand with your left thumb directly over your right thumb. No part of your right hand should touch the grip. Now, make your chipping stoke.

WHAT IT DOES

This right-over-left-hand grip removes your right arm from your stroke, making your chip swing a left-arm-dominated motion. This is a good thing, since it's critical that your left arm never stop moving through the shot. If your left arm ever stops moving toward the target on your forward-swing, the clubhead will flip past your hands and you'll catch the shot fat or thin.

Place left hand on middle of grip...

...then place right hand over left.

Hit a few chips with this "claw" grip, then go back to your normal hold. You should feel like your left arm is dominating your stroke, and finish with your left arm in front of your left leg. If you still can't do it, go back to the claw, then lower one finger at a time on the handle until you can translate the feel to your regular grip. Or, use the claw when you play. If it helps you to keep your left arm moving, you'll become a more consistent chipper.

The claw grip teaches you proper left-arm action.

TOP 100 TEACHER POLL

Q What's the most damaging error amateurs make when chipping?

Clubhead passing the hands—66%

Poor ball position—12%

Overswinging—22%

"You need momentum to chip well. You lose it when you allow the clubhead to pass your hands at the bottom of your swing."
—Top 100 Teacher Kellie Stenzel

SHOTMAKING

Make Your Chips Bite

You want spin? Here's how to get it.

—Top 100 Teacher Scott Sackett

THIS STORY IS FOR YOU IF...

1
Your chips tend to roll too far.

2
You can't spin your chips—any wedge shot for that matter.

THE PROBLEM

You never hit the ball crisp enough to put spin on the ball, so your chips almost always tend to roll out too far. You'd like your chips to take a couple of hops, then settle quick—and close to the hole.

WHY IT'S HAPPENING

Like most golfers, you're too caught up in controlling the direction you hit your chips—you think you have to swing your wedge straight down the target line. That works in some instances, but it will never give you the spin control that makes getting up and down easy.

THE SOLUTION

As you swing through impact, move your arms to the left of the target. Don't make a viscious cut across the ball, but rather a smooth swing around your body in your follow-through. This creates a more dynamic impact, allowing the grooves on your wedge's face to grab the ball and impart the shot-stopping spin you're looking for. For even more spin, take the club back slightly to the inside, then really swing your hands and arms left after impact.

NO SPIN
Clubhead swings straight down the target line after impact

HIGH SPIN
Clubhead swings left of the target line after impact.

How to Chip It Close

Land the ball one pace on and let your club selection take care of the rest

—*Top 100 Teacher Scott Sackett*

THIS STORY IS FOR YOU IF...

1
You're confused by how much carry and roll you need to land chips close.

2
You hit every chip with your sand wedge.

THE PROBLEM

You're aware that every chip shot you hit features varying amounts of carry and roll, but you don't know how to select clubs or adjust your swing to get the right combination for the shot you're facing.

THE SOLUTION

Regardless of how far off the green the ball is sitting, or where the pin is positioned, try to land every chip one pace on the front edge of the green. That gives you a baseline for determining the exact amount of carry versus roll for every shot. Then, using the guide at right, pull the club that's designed to produce that particular ratio. With the correct club in your hand, just make the swing you think will land the ball one pace on the green. This works for any distance and any pin position from good lies around the green.

Determine the yards needed to land the ball one pace on (carry), and the yards from the front edge to the cup (roll), then pull the appropriate club based on the chart below.

Club Guide (Carry:Roll)

< 2:1	LOB WEDGE
2:1	SAND WEDGE
1:1	PITCH WEDGE
1:2	9-IRON
1:3	8-IRON
1:4	7-IRON
>1:5	6-IRON

HOW TO GET THE RIGHT COMBINATION OF CARRY AND ROLL

Say you're 3 paces from a spot that's 1 pace onto the green, and the pin is another 12 paces from the spot. Dividing 12 by 3 gives you 4, which is the carry-to-roll ratio for the chip (3 paces of carry, 12 paces of roll). Checking the club-selection guide above, that's 7-iron. If the pin was only 6 paces from the spot you'd hit a 9-iron.

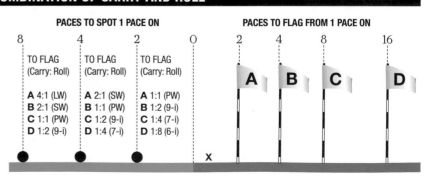

PACES TO SPOT 1 PACE ON

8	4	2	0
TO FLAG (Carry: Roll)	TO FLAG (Carry: Roll)	TO FLAG (Carry: Roll)	
A 4:1 (LW)	**A** 2:1 (SW)	**A** 1:1 (PW)	
B 2:1 (SW)	**B** 1:1 (PW)	**B** 1:2 (9-i)	
C 1:1 (PW)	**C** 1:2 (9-i)	**C** 1:4 (7-i)	
D 1:2 (9-i)	**D** 1:4 (7-i)	**D** 1:8 (6-i)	

PACES TO FLAG FROM 1 PACE ON

2	4	8	16
A	B	C	D

SHOTMAKING

Chip From The Rough

You missed the green. Big deal! Here's how to make par anyway.

—*Top 100 Teacher Mike Adams*

THIS STORY IS FOR YOU IF...

1
You're an expert chipper...

2
...as long as the ball is sitting on the short stuff.

THE SITUATION
Your approach shot missed the green by only a few yards and the ball is in the rough, but not too deep. However, you're not sure your regular pitching motion will create clean contact and allow you to leave the ball near the hole.

THE SOLUTION
Use your regular pitch swing, but make it steeper (to get the ball out) and vary your stance and grip (to move the ball the right distance). Here's how.

Square the leading edge to your target so you have more clubface area to strike the ball (opening the face reduces contact area).

STEP 1
Address the ball like normal and then stand back from it a little (feel like your hands are lower than usual and in a pre-cocked position). This adds bounce to the club (to help push it through the rough).

STEP 2
Hinge your wrists to trigger your backswing, then make your regular chip motion with about 75 percent force. At impact, feel like the club is slipping under the ball and popping it more up than forward.

HOW TO

Chip With The Ball Above Your Feet

Change your setup so you don't catch this one fat

—Top 100 Teacher Donald Crawley

THIS STORY IS FOR YOU IF...

1
Your course features severe mounding around greens.

2
You catch chips fat.

THE SITUATION
Your ball landed just short of the green, but within easy chipping distance of the pin. When you go to take your stance, however, the ball is significantly above your feet.

HOW THE SLOPE AFFECTS YOU
Since the ball is above your feet, the lie of your club is flatter, and a flatter lie usually translates to a closed clubface. This ball wants to go left. And since your chest is closer to the ball than when it's sitting on flat ground, the tendency is for your swing to bottom out too far underneath your lie, leading to fat contact.

THE SOLUTION
Whenever you're on any kind of slope (as you'll read about on these pages and the following six), you have to make certain adjustments to offset the effects of the hill, or your contact, distance control and scores will suffer. Tweaking your normal setup and swing technique is more than enough to compensate for the slope and get the job done.

HOW TO OFFSET THE SLOPE

● **Posture:** Stand taller (less forward bend and less knee flex) or choke down on the club until the sole rests on the ground with its original lie angle intact.
● **Ball Position:** Standard.
● **Aim:** Slightly to the right of your target, since the effects of the slope will pull the ball left, or...
● ...aim at your target, and open the clubface a few degrees.

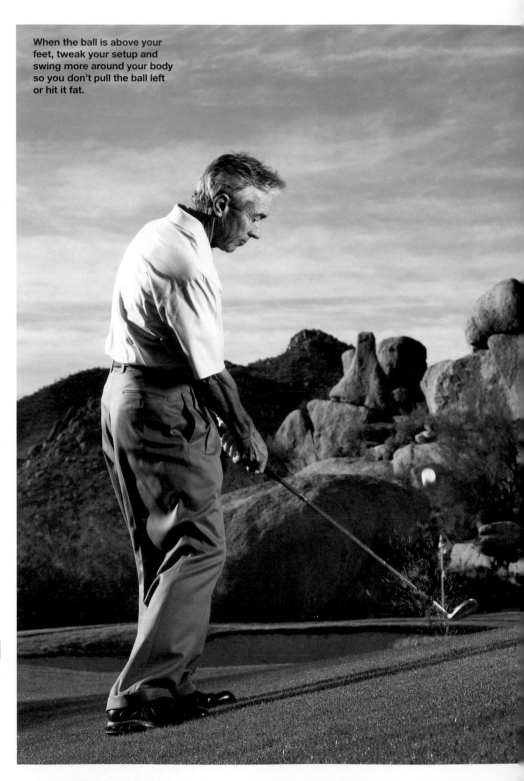

When the ball is above your feet, tweak your setup and swing more around your body so you don't pull the ball left or hit it fat.

HOW TO CHIP IT CRISP WHEN THE BALL IS ABOVE YOUR FEET

1 Try to create your standard address. Stand closer and grip down if you feel your posture is too upright.

2 The slope creates a naturally flatter swing plane. Don't fight it.

3 Feel like the club is more behind you. Remember, your swing plane is tilted because of the slope.

4 Focus on balance. Gravity wants to pull you back. Keep your chest over the ball.

5 If your setup is correct, you'll make the same crisp contact that you do when the lie is flat.

6 Keep the flat-plane theme going in your forward-swing. Swing left of the target, not at the target.

QUICK TIP
Make a few practice swings before hitting the shot. Make them in succession, brushing the grass both back and through. It will give you the confidence you need when you go to hit the shot for real.

HOW TO

Chip With The Ball Below Your Feet

This one's easy to catch thin. Here's how to catch it crisp

—*Top 100 Teacher Donald Crawley*

THIS STORY IS FOR YOU IF...

1

You don't feel comfortable when you have to reach for the ball, like you do when it's below your feet.

THE SITUATION

Your ball landed just short of the green within easy chipping distance of the pin. When you go to take your stance, however, the ball is significantly below your feet. You get the feeling that you're going to blade this one across the green.

HOW THE SLOPE AFFECTS YOU

Since the ball is below your feet, the lie of your club is more upright, and a more upright lie usually translates to an open clubface. This ball wants to go right. And since the ball is farther from your chest than it is when it's sitting on flat ground, the tendency is for your swing to bottom out above ball, leading to thin shots and skulls.

THE SOLUTION

Just like you did when the ball was above your feet *[page 128]*, the secret to pulling off this shot is to offset how the slope affects your stance and your swing path by altering your setup position.

HOW TO OFFSET THE SLOPE

● **Posture:** Stand less tall by bending your knees more (don't over-bend from your hips). Or...
● ...try standing a little closer to the ball. This will make the shaft even more upright—that's okay, because this swing needs to be a little more vertical than what you're used to.
● **Ball Position:** Standard
● **Aim:** Slightly to the left of your target, since the effects of the slope will pull the ball right, or...
● ...aim at your target, and hood the clubface a few degrees.

When the ball sits below your feet, simple adjustments to your setup will allow you to make a more vertical swing so you don't catch the ball thin.

HOW TO CHIP IT CRISP WHEN THE BALL IS BELOW YOUR FEET

1 Notice how the downslope sets me up to swing more up and down, and less around my body.

2 Keep your knees flexed and your chest over the ball. It's easy to lift up out of your posture from this lie.

3 A very vertical backswing will help you get all the way back down to the ball on your downswing.

4 Try to create the same steep path you made going back as you bring the clubhead back to the ball.

5 Don't chop at impact. Keep it smooth and let your more vertical chip swing path take care of the rest.

6 Feel like your weight is a bit more in your heels than usual. This will help you maintain balance.

QUICK TIP
Keep your eyes focused on the ball. If you peek too early on this shot, you'll increase the likelihood of catching the ball thin.

From a downslope, play the ball back in your stance to offset the fact that the bottom of your swing arc occurs earlier than when you have a flat lie.

HOW TO

Chip On a Downslope

Choose more loft so you don't run this one past the hole

—Top 100 Teacher Donald Crawley

THIS STORY IS FOR YOU IF...

1
You have distance-control problems on sloping lies.

2
You play courses with severe elevation changes.

THE SITUATION
Your ball landed just short of the green. When you go to take your stance, your left foot is significantly below your right foot, and this makes you feel very uncomfortable.

HOW THE SLOPE AFFECTS YOU
When you're on a flat lie, there's a specific point where your swing bottoms out, and that's usually where you want to position the ball in your stance. What happens when you're on a downslope is that the bottom of your swing arc moves back, since the ground behind the ball is higher than the ground in front of the ball.

THE SOLUTION
Unlike the situations where you're chipping with the ball above *[page 128]* and below *[page 130]* your feet, the slope in this situation is working in the direction of where you want the ball to go. This places a premium on ball position. Get it wrong here and you'll hit the shot fat and short, or thin it to the other side of the green.

HOW TO OFFSET THE SLOPE

● **Posture:** Standard.
● **Ball Position:** Play it in the middle, or a ball or two back of center to match it up with the bottom of your swing.
● **Aim:** At target.
● **Club Selection:** A downslope typically removes loft from your clubface, since your swing path is deeper compared to the line of flight. You'll have to hit this one a little softer, or select a higher-lofted club.

HOW TO CHIP IT CRISP FROM A DOWNSLOPE

1

Use your normal chipping setup, but favor a middle ball position, or even back of middle.

2

Judging by the slope and the position of my hands, it's easy to see how the club will bottom early.

3

Get a feeling that you're swinging down the slope, not necessarily into the back of the ball.

4

The ball will come off lower and roll a little more than usual, so plan your landing point carefully.

5

Continue swinging down the slope. It's easy to do if you lead your downswing with your left arm.

6

You'll know you did it right if your clubhead finishes low to the ground.

QUICK TIP
Instead of fighting the slope, go with it. As you bring the club into the ball, allow your lower body to lean down the hill and toward the target. This will keep you from jabbing at the ball, and you'll make a more rhythmic stroke.

Guarantee crisp contact when chipping up a hill by adjusting for the fact that your swing will naturally bottom out in front of its usual spot.

HOW TO

Chip From an Upslope

The tendency here is to come up short
—*Top 100 Teacher Donald Crawley*

THE SITUATION

Your ball landed just short of the green. When you go to take your stance, your right foot is significantly below your left foot. You fell like you can't make good contact unless you seriously alter your swing. Worse yet, you don't know which adjustments to make.

HOW THE SLOPE AFFECTS YOU

It's forcing you to swing up on the ball relative to its line of flight, which, as you can guess, is going to add extra loft to the shot regardless of the club you pull from your bag. You can go with the club you'd use from the same distance on a flat lie, but you'll have to give it extra oomph.

THE SOLUTION

Just like the downslope situation *[page 132]*, the slope is working in the direction of your swing and is affecting the natural bottom of your swing arc. This time, the slope is causing your swing to bottom out in front of its usual spot. You need to play the ball forward or you'll hit the shot thin.

HOW TO OFFSET THE SLOPE

● **Posture:** Standard.
● **Ball Position:** Play it one or two balls forward in your stance (toward your left foot), depending on the severity of the slope.
● **Aim:** At target.
● **Club selection:** If you want to make the same size chip swing you'd use from this distance on a flat lie, select one more club. The extra loft created by the upslope will add loft and subtract distance.

HOW TO CHIP IT CRISP FROM AN UPSLOPE

1 Tip your shoulders just enough so that they match the angle of the slope.

2 Make your normal move away from the ball, being careful not to slide away from the target.

3 Very little hinge. Making a steep swing will increase the chances of jamming the club into the hill.

4 Try to swing up the slope. You don't have to overdo it—just get a nice feeling of swinging along the hill.

5 Kink in your right knee just a tad. Notice how this shortens my right side, helping me swing up the hill.

6 The ball will come off with a higher trajectory than normal. Continue tracking the clubhead up the hill.

QUICK TIP
You may not be used to playing the ball forward in your stance, so make a good three to four practice swings before attempting a chip from an upslope. Picture the higher trajectory in your mind's eye, then smoothly pull the trigger.

Most players think of sand shots as penalty strokes, but it doesn't have to be that way. With the right fundamentals and a few key swing thoughts, your sand game can become a legitimate scoring game.

7

SAND SHOTS
MADE EASY

Learn the proven skills—and a few new tricks—to get out of any bunker and close to the pin on your first swing

BEAT THE BUNKER BLUES

Yes, bunkers are penalty zones. They're there for a reason: To make you pay for an errant shot. But when you think of all the other nasty places your ball can find when it flies astray off the face of your driver and irons, the sand actually isn't a bad place to be. Good golfers excel in sand, and are able to get the ball up and on the green a good percentage of the time. This is because the techniques for escaping the sand aren't that difficult, especially when you compare them to the demands of your full swing and other short-game plays. Once you get the basics down, almost any sand shot becomes easy. With the Top 100 Teachers as your guide, you'll start to look forward to hitting from the sand, instead of fearing the worst.

Your Basic Bunker Shot

To get the ball out of the sand you need to get sand out of the bunker

—Top 100 Teacher Mike Malaska

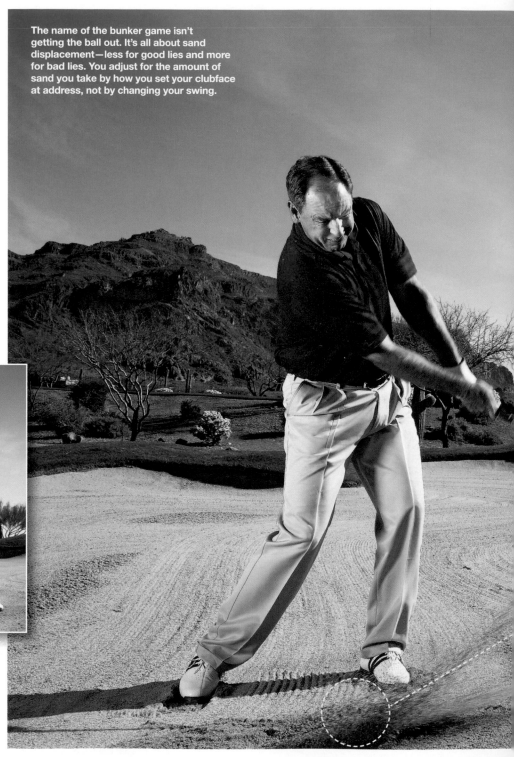

The name of the bunker game isn't getting the ball out. It's all about sand displacement—less for good lies and more for bad lies. You adjust for the amount of sand you take by how you set your clubface at address, not by changing your swing.

THIS STORY IS FOR YOU IF...

1
You rarely get out of bunkers on your first swing...

2
...and sometimes your second.

THE PROBLEM

You're vexed by bunkers. You're not really sure how you should address the ball in sand, how hard to swing your sand wedge or where to make contact. Truth is, you're making things hard on yourself by over-thinking the situation. All good bunker players know that the secret to getting the ball out of sand is getting sand out of the bunker.

THE SOLUTION

Simplify your sand woes by taking your normal stance and making your full, normal swing. The only key adjustment is to open your clubface when the ball is sitting up, square it if the ball is partly submerged, and hood it if the ball is buried. Each of these clubface positions allows you to displace varying amounts of sand when your club enters and swings through the bunker. An open face takes less sand; a closed face takes more.

All you really need to concern yourself with is hitting behind the ball and taking the right amount of sand for the shot at hand, which you do by changing the position of your clubface (open, square or closed). The ball goes where the sand goes, and the sand goes in the direction of your swing, not where your clubface is pointed.

Make a full backswing on every bunker shot. If you set your clubface correctly and hit behind the ball, you'll take the correct amount of sand to launch the ball up and onto the green.

OPEN THE FACE

When the ball is sitting up. This allows your wedge to skid more than dig and take less sand. The ball will go in the direction of the sand, not where your clubface is aimed.

SQUARE THE FACE

When the ball is partly submerged. This allows the leading edge of your sand wedge to dig into the bunker a little deeper and take more sand than when the face is open.

CLOSE THE FACE

When the ball is buried. This allows the toe of your sand wedge to really dig into the bunker and displace a lot of sand. Don't worry, the ball won't go left.

Normal setup and address with your clubface angled (set open, square or closed) to match the lie.

Don't go after trick pins. Your goal is to get the ball on and then two-putt.

Full hinge and shoulder turn. As soon as you shorten your swing, your chances of success go kaput.

Notice how everything is moving toward the bunker, not lifting away from it.

Swing along your toe line. The sand and the ball will fly in the direction you align your body and swing.

Club enters the sand, and takes varying amounts depending on how you angle the clubface at address.

WATCH & LEARN

The Basic Bunker Shot

Copy these positions to get the ball up and out on your first swing
—*Top 100 Teacher Mike Malaska*

IT'S A SWING IN FULL

If you're like most golfers, you're afraid to make a big swing in sand because the ball might fly too far. After all, you're right next to the green, and a full swing is *waaaaaay* too much power, right? Wrong. This is one of the few times in golf where you're actually required to hit too far behind the ball. Your target at the bottom of your swing is the sand,

4 Don't worry about hitting the shot too far. Your goal is to knock sand out of the bunker, not the ball.

5 Think of pulling the club down into the sand with your left arm.

6 Use a little less leg action than normal to improve your stability in the sand.

10 The sand lifts the ball out of the bunker, not the club. This is the essential theme for any sand shot.

11 Picture the club striking the sand behind the ball, and exiting the sand in front of the ball.

12 Full finish. Aim at the center of the green if the pin is in a tight spot. Your goal is to two-putt.

not the ball itself. Another reason why you need to make a full swing in the bunker is that sand is heavy. On most bunker shots you'll displace a full cupful of sand. That's a significant amount of weight, which is why you need to free up your backswing and come down with good acceleration to launch the sand and the ball out of the bunker. If you cut your backswing short or slow down as

your clubhead approaches impact, you'll likely be hitting your next shot from the sand, too.

Remember, you don't have to get yourself caught up in tricky setup positions. The techniques discussed here will do the trick for 90 percent of the bunker shots you'll face during the normal course of play. That's a good head start in turning what's normally a penalty situation into a save.

> **"The ball goes where the sand goes, not where your clubface is pointed."**

TECHNIQUE

Set Up For Sand Success

Fine-tune your address position to take advantage of your natural swing

—Top 100 Teacher Kellie Stenzel

THIS STORY IS FOR YOU IF...

1
You see golfers open their stance in the sand...

2
...and aren't sure if you should too.

CHECK THIS!

As with anything in golf, there's more than one way to get the job done in a bunker, especially where your setup is concerned. You don't have to do anything special with your stance— you can set up square just like you do in the fairway when trying to hit a straight shot into the green. The only reason you see people aim to the left of the flag in sand is because they've probably opened their clubface and are attempting to hit a cut shot. That's usually a little more trouble than it's worth, but for some golfers, an open stance works better than a square one in sand. Check the guide at right to discover which type of setup will work best with your natural swing.

If you're a slow swinger, or you tend to slice the ball...

SET UP SQUARE

Aim your sand wedge at your target, and set your feet parallel left of your target line. When you go to swing, swing along your target line.

WHY IT WORKS

Slicers tend to open the face too much at impact. If you set up with your feet pointed left and the face open to your swing line, you could experience disastrous results. Low swing-speed players need as much power as possible in sand, and opening the face usually results in a higher, shorter shot.

WATCH OUT!

Since many golfers don't really know what a square clubface looks like at address (even though they think they do), use the marks on your grip—not the leading edge—to make sure you don't unduly set the clubface open or closed.

If you're a high-swing-speed player, or you tend to hook the ball…

SET UP OPEN

Align your body slightly left of your target and set your clubface square to the target. Your clubface should look open to you.

WHY IT WORKS

When you swing fast, you hit the ball far, so opening your clubface relative to your stance (and swing) line can give you better distance control in bunkers. The open face will give you a higher, softer shot. If you hook, setting the face open at address means there's less chance that the face will be closed at impact, like it is if you pull the ball.

WATCH OUT!

When players open their stance in the sand, they usually do so after they've set their ball position. But notice how opening up your stance moves the ball position back *[top photo]*. Set your left foot first, then your right, and you'll do a better job of keeping the ball around the middle of your stance *[bottom photo]*.

TRY THIS!

Be on your toes in the sand

If you struggle from the sand, there's a good chance you're hanging back on your right side through the ball in an attempt to scoop it. The upward motion leaves only the tiniest margin for error, and if you don't make perfect impact you'll hit the shot fat or blade it across the green.

Instead of hanging back, set up with your weight favoring your left side and leave it there throughout your swing, and rotate your hips so that your body turns toward the target at impact. It's like tossing a softball—your hips turn out of the way before you let go of the ball. Turning your hips creates a downward blow that carries the ball out of the bunker on a cushion of sand with a much larger margin for error.

To ingrain the proper turn, hit practice sand shots with your right foot pulled back and up on its toes. This will keep you from sliding to the right and will force your hips to turn toward the target on the downswing. Now you're rotating over your left leg on the downswing, rather than falling back onto your right leg.

Hitting practice shots with your right foot pulled back on its toes will force your hips to turn toward the target on the downswing.

The Secret to Great Bunker Shots

When you keep the face from closing, your chances for success go through the roof

—*Top 100 Teacher Mike LaBauve*

THIS STORY IS FOR YOU IF...
1 You're a "handsy" sand player.
2 You think you need to release the club when hitting bunker shots.

CHECK THIS!

Do you want to know the real secret to hitting consistently successful sand shots? If so, check the two swing sequences at right. They appear very similar, but if you look closely you'll see a subtle difference in the clubface as it swings through and exits the sand.

WHAT YOU'RE LOOKING AT

Clubface rotation through impact. Notice in the bottom sequence of photos how the face of the sand wedge stays open all the way through the sand. You can grill pancakes on this clubface and not spill an ounce of batter! In the top sequence, the face is rotating—you can see how much less loft there is on the club as it moves through the sand. This type of clubface rotation is good for full swings from the fairway and tee box, but not in the sand. Your goal for most bunker shots is to keep the face from shutting down, which allows the sole of the club and the bounce angle to help your wedge glide through the sand and not dig in too deeply.

NO The clubface is turning only a little at this point, but it's turning nonetheless. With more leading edge, more sand is displaced than below.

Taking more sand means a slower swing speed through impact. Notice the difference in height between the two balls.

YES When you keep the face from rotating through impact, you allow the sole of the club to glide through the sand that's under the ball.

The club exits the bunker with the same amount of loft it started with at address. You get the feeling that the sole struck the sand, not the leading edge. Perfect.

You can start to see the underside of the club—evidence that the face is rotating. You're really losing loft and ball speed now.

The ball isn't riding on a cushion of sand, it's riding *in* a cushion of sand. The benefits of the loft built into your sand wedge are gone.

This is a great clubhead position for a full swing, where you want to release the club, but this ball is going to come up short.

When you use your wedge correctly, it creates a cushion of sand that propels the ball up and out. The sand is propelling the ball skyward.

Even this deep into the swing, the face is still flat—zero hand manipulation. The ball is up and on its way to the green.

Swing your arms, not your hands, to keep the face from shutting down. If you can hold the face steady through impact, you'll get the ball out every time.

How to Hack It From Sand

Forget the splash technique and do a cannonball instead

—*Top 100 Teacher Dr. Gary Wiren*

THIS STORY IS FOR YOU IF...

1
You're hopeless— nothing helps your sand game.
2
You want to pound those stupid bunkers!

THE PROBLEM

When you try to make a sand swing like you're taught, you almost always thin the ball. You never take enough sand, and don't quite understand the "splash-it-out" theory.

THE SOLUTION

Your only goal in a bunker is to hit the sand behind the ball and let the dislodged material push it out. If that's the case, then you don't have to worry about what you do underneath the ball, but behind it. If you're looking for an easy way to get out of bunkers, grab your wedge, make a big swing and go pound sand.

HOW TO HACK IT FROM THE SAND

Take your normal setup, but with a less-lofted iron (like a pitching wedge) and play the ball back in your stance.

Make a full backswing. Really load up your wrists, but be careful not to overswing.

3

Aim for a spot behind the ball and give that bunker a beating! Don't worry about what happens after impact—just bury your club in the sand. Since you've chosen less loft, you'll dig deep and dislodge enough sand to carry the ball out.

DRILL

Draw Your Way to Easy Sand Escapes

The quadrant sand method works wonders for both the bunker-skilled and the bunker-challenged

—Top 100 Teacher Dr. T.J. Tomasi

THIS STORY IS FOR YOU IF...

1
You understand the principles of the basic sand shot...

2
but that doesn't mean it always translates to your swing.

TRY THIS!
The next time you're in a practice bunker, draw two perpendicular lines in the sand, with one of the lines pointing at your target. Place a ball where the lines intersect and, from your perspective behind the ball, draw numbers in each of the four quadrants using the butt of your sand wedge. Draw the number "1" in the top-left quadrant, then move clockwise to number the remaining quadrants (2, 3 and 4).

This is the opposite of your normal swing, where you want to move the club from quadrant 4 to quadrant 2 (inside-out path). In sand, however, swinging from quadrant 3 to 1 is the fast track to easy escapes.

Open stance.

Right foot in quadrant 4.

Clubface square to target.

SETUP
Address the ball by placing your right foot in quadrant 4, and your left foot on the line running perpendicular to your target line. Pull your left foot back a full foot's width. This sets you up open to your target line. Set the leading edge of your club square to the line running to your target.

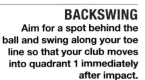

Swing back to quadrant 3.

BACKSWING
Swing your clubhead into quadrant 3. If you've had bunker problems in the past, you've probably been swinging the club back into quadrant 4.

Swing through to quadrant 1.

BACKSWING
Aim for a spot behind the ball and swing along your toe line so that your club moves into quadrant 1 immediately after impact.

How to Practice Your Bunker Fundamentals

These three drills quickly fix the flaws that cause your bunker shots to fail

—Top 100 Teacher Bill Davis

THE SITUATION

You don't know what part of your sand game needs work, but you know it's in need of repair. You don't mind practicing, but could use a few drills to give your sand practice some structure. Here are three excellent ones.

DRILL 1

SPLIT-GRIP SWINGS

Fixes: Poor bunker-swing mechanics

Step into a practice bunker and plop a ball in the sand. Take your normal address position, but separate your hands on the handle so that your left thumb just touches the pad of your right hand. This split grip helps you learn three bunker fundamentals (wrist hinge, arm swing, and clubhead control), that when applied correctly make escaping the sand and knocking the ball close easy.

FEEL THE POWER

With your hands separated on the handle, they'll be harder to rotate. This helps you keep the face from unduly rotating through impact and taking too much sand.

FEEL THE MOMENTUM

The split grip encourages an arm-dominated swing with minimal lower-body movement. Things get dicey when you add too much leg action. Turn smoothly toward the target and let your arms do the bulk of the work.

FEEL THE HINGE

As you take the club back, notice how the split grip causes your wrists to hinge quickly and fully, with your left hand pushing out on the handle. Hinging your wrists like this allows you to hit down into the sand so that the club can pass under the ball.

DRILL 2

DIVOT FINDER

Fixes: Hitting too close to the ball or too far behind the ball

Take your normal setup position. As you do, notice how you automatically set the club directly behind the ball. No wonder you can't hit the sand behind it! You're setting yourself up for a skull even before you start, especially if you're not very skilled at taking consistent sand divots.

Make everything else the same, but set your club a good six inches behind the ball at address. This sets you in better position to hit behind the ball and sweep sand from underneath it. Try it in the practice bunker a few times. It works like a charm—so good you may choose to use it when you make bunker swings on the course.

YES

Start here...

NO

...instead of here.

DRILL 3

SAND SPLASHES

Fixes: Using sand to carry the ball out of the bunker, not your club

One of the reasons recreational players struggle in bunkers is that they're not familiar with the sand getting in the way, or with the fact that the ball goes where the sand goes. That's an important piece of the bunker-shot puzzle—you must learn to hit the sand toward your target.

Build up a good pile of sand on top of the bunker's surface and play it like it's the ball. Don't make a backswing—start at address and sling your club forward. Your goal is to push the sand toward your target (you'll push it left or right of your target at first). Once you get good with just sand, drop a ball in the bunker and try to create the same feeling in your through-swing.

1

Without taking a backswing...

2

...sling the sand toward your target.

SOLID TURN

If you think that the sand swing is an arms-only swing, think again. Look at the way Tiger rotates his upper body through impact—his chest is pointing directly at the target. This is a good move to copy for all bunker shots. As soon as you stop turning your body, the clubhead will flip past your hands, giving you plenty of bunker misery and unnecessary strokes.

FACE OPEN

It may look like Tiger's clubface has rotated closed, but that's only because he's swinging his right arm across his chest and the clubhead to the left of his target. It's actually fairly open— a good move in sand to keep your clubhead from digging too deeply into the bunker and hitting the shot too short.

SAND AT TARGET

This is a great image of how the ball is propelled out of the bunker by the sand, not the clubhead. Another lesson you can learn from this snapshot is how both the sand and the ball are traveling in the same direction. In a standard bunker shot, the ball goes where the sand goes, and the sand travels in the direction of your swing, not in the direction your clubface is pointed at address.

Tiger Woods

Tiger isn't truly superhuman; he still finds bunkers and misses greens just like you do. Unlike you, however—and unlike the collective field at a Tour event—he walks away with par or better when his approach shot misses the green almost two-thirds of the time. Obviously, Tiger doesn't plan on missing greens, but he does plan on where to leave a bad approach in case he does. Tiger scrambles better not because his technique is better (his competition includes scores of world-class escape artists), but because he thinks about the best place to leave a bad approach. He's always thinking. He plays like a poker ace—he's always at least several moves ahead of the field.

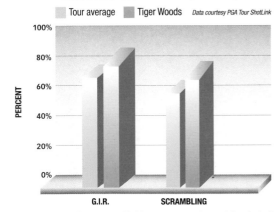

TIGER WOODS' SCORING SECRET (2002-2008)

Tour average · Tiger Woods · *Data courtesy PGA Tour ShotLink*

Tiger scores in two different ways: He hits more greens in regulation (so he has more birdie chances) and he scrambles at a higher rate (so he can miss greens and still keep his scores in the red).

SHOTMAKING

Blast It Extra-High

Use this quirky setup to get the ball up, up into the air
—*Top 100 Teacher Scott Sackett*

THIS STORY IS FOR YOU IF...
1
You don't know how to vary trajectory from the sand.
2
Your course features a lot of deep bunkers.

THE SITUATION

You're in a deep greenside bunker, and your standard bunker trajectory probably won't clear the lip. Or, you're in a regular-depth greenside bunker, but the pin is cut very close to the fringe in front of you. You need a lob shot, not a sand shot.

THE SMART PLAY

Use your lob wedge instead of your sand wedge. The extra loft will come in handy in those situations where you need an extra-high shot out of the bunker. For the times you need even more loft, use this special setup to add those few extra degrees of loft so you can clear the lip when you're really down deep.

> "The more sand you take underneath the ball, the higher it will fly."

HOW TO DO IT

1 Take your normal sand setup, playing the ball slightly forward of your stance, and open the face a few degrees.

2 Spread your feet so that they're outside your shoulders and buckle your knees inward, like you're stepping onto a rink with ice skates for the first time. Kink in your right knee a little more than your left, so that your body tilts at a small angle.

3 Make your everyday swing. Lowering your stance lowers the bottom of your swing arc, so you displace more sand underneath the ball. That mass of sand pushes the ball up more than it does out. Give it a good swing—you'll need some extra gas to carry the ball the distance you need.

Make the Ball Sit or Run

Change the way your club exits the sand to add spin or roll the ball up to the flag
—*Top 100 Teacher Scott Sackett*

THE PROBLEM

You're getting your bunker shots on the green, but they often hit and then run past the hole like they owe it money.

THE SOLUTION

Sometimes having the ball hit and run is the right play, like when you have lots of green to work with. But on most sand shots, adding spin is the easy way to keep the ball within one-putt range. Good players have both shots.

HOW TO RUN IT UP CLOSE
Finish using a shortened version of your regular full swing, with your body facing the target and your right arm stretched across your torso.

HOW TO MAKE IT BITE
Quickly lift the club out of the sand by bending your left elbow after impact. It should feel like you're trying to get the shaft straight up and down as soon as you strike the sand.

NOTE: The difference between the two shots is that your wedge exits the sand on a shallow angle when you don't want spin, and on a more vertical angle when you need extra spin to stop the ball close to the hole.

Picture a Perfect Weight Shift

It's the difference between a successful shot and a skull

—*Top 100 Teacher Bill Forrest*

THIS STORY IS FOR YOU IF...
1
You focus mostly on your arms when you swing in sand.
2
You catch a lot of bunker shots thin.

PICTURE THIS!

Regardless of any move you make in your bunker swing, or whatever sand-swing technique you adhere to, you must start with your weight left, and rotate more weight to the left.

When you swing like this *[sequence, right]* your club automatically bottoms out in the center of your stance. Now you can adjust the ball position based on the sand. If you're in soft, heavy sand, move the ball forward in your stance four inches to splash out a lot of sand with the ball. But if you're on wet, hard sand, keep the ball in the center and hit it and the ground at the same time. Always hit the sand first with the bounce of the club, not the leading edge.

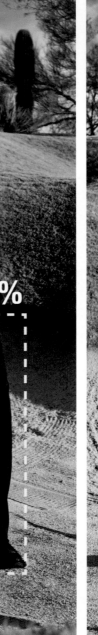

55%

1

ADDRESS
Start with about 55 percent of your weight on your left side.

55%

2

BACKSWING
As you swing the club back, keep that weight over your left side. No shifting or swaying!

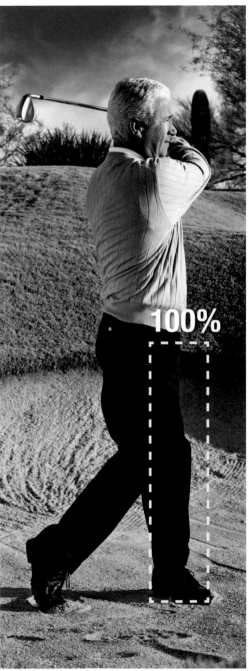

3

THROUGH IMPACT
Rotate even more of your weight to the left side.

4

FINISH
At the end of your swing, all of your weight should be on your left side.

FROM THE *GM* VAULT

How to Solve the Sand
By PGA Tour player Bob Charles
GOLF Magazine, December 1965

One of the big reasons for missed trap shots is slipping during the swing. Dig in well with both feet as you take your stance, so that you get as firm a foundation for your swing as possible. And keep your left heel down in the sand as you swing back. If you lift it on your backswing, it likely won't return to the same place on your downswing, which can cause fatal inaccuracy.

"Don't keep your eye on the ball. Fix your gaze on a spot in the sand behind the ball, and keep it there during your swing."
—Bob Charles

DRILL

How to Take the Right-Size Divot

This drill stops fat and thin bunker shots in their tracks

—*Top 100 Teacher Laird Small*

THIS STORY IS FOR YOU IF...

1
You're taking sand but still hitting the ball thin.

2
You don't know how much sand to take from the bunker.

THE FAULT
You struggle in bunkers because you usually enter the sand too far behind the ball. This means that your club exits the sand at the ball and fails to take the sand directly underneath it, which the ball needs to ride on to exit the bunker. You know this is happening to you if you often leave your first attempt in the bunker. Sometimes you may even hit so far behind the ball that the club exits before it. That's when you end up skulling the ball over the green.

THE FIX
Try the "Umbrella Drill." It's the easiest way to learn how to make contact with the sand in the right spot and float the ball close to the pin.

STEP 1
Draw a line in the sand that arcs around your body. Think of this line as an umbrella. Draw a second line from the center of the umbrella—this is the umbrella's handle. Position the ball on the handle line and take your stance (with the ball positioned just forward of center).

STEP 2
Once you're set, swing your arms along the umbrella line. You'll notice that as your arms swing in the direction of the arc on the way back to the ball, they pull your sternum over the handle of the umbrella. This forward body move allows you to enter the sand closer to the ball and exit the sand in front of the ball, taking the perfect-size divot to float the ball onto the green.

Swing the club along the arc.

Enter the sand here.

Exit the sand here.

SHOTMAKING

Blast It Short or Long

Control the distance of your bunker shots by changing your finish, not your backswing

—*Top 100 Teacher Eden Foster*

THE PROBLEM

When you do manage to get out of the sand on your first swing, the ball never lands close to the hole, making it difficult to save par.

THE SOLUTION

The trick is to match how you release the club to the distance you're facing—everything else in your bunker swing should stay the same.

Finish below your waist for short bunker shots.

Finish above your waist for long bunker shots.

FOR BUNKER SHOTS OF LESS THAN 10 YARDS...

...make an abbreviated finish with your hands stopping below waist height. As you do this, keep your right arm from turning over your left so you don't release the club like you do on your regular full swing. Notice how this non-release keeps the clubface open and creates a softer ball flight. The softer the shot, the shorter the distance it will carry.

FOR BUNKER SHOTS LONGER THAN 10 YARDS...

...release the club like you do when you're hitting approach shots from the fairway. You don't need a full finish. What's important is that you release the clubhead so that your left palm faces the sky. You know you're doing it right if the clubhead finishes high above your hands. This type of release adds extra oomph to your sand swing, helping you to fly the ball all the way to the hole.

A full swing from a bunker typically generates 50 percent of the distance you get from the same club in the fairway.

Change Clubs to Blast Close

Simple math helps you select the right club for the shot at hand

—Top 100 Teacher John Elliott Jr.

THIS STORY IS FOR YOU IF...

1
You don't have good distance control out of bunkers.

2
You use sand wedge for almost every bunker swing.

THE PROBLEM

Some bunkers feature heavy sand, others are filled with fluffy sand. Sometimes there's a lot of it, and other times you feel like you're playing off hardpan. This makes it difficult to determine how far a given bunker shot will fly, and one of the reasons why bunkers are there in the first place—you're meant to be paying for an errant shot.

THE SOLUTION

Your goal is to get on the green. If you get close, great. This actually takes pressure off your short game—you don't need to be ultra-exact with your distances. As a rule, a swing from a bunker will fly the ball roughly half as far as the same swing with the same club in the fairway. Another good rule to follow: don't fall in love with your sand wedge. Your other wedges, even your 9-iron, can work wonders in sand, and get you close from any distance from 75 yards and in *[see table, below]*.

FULL-SWING DISTANCES

CLUB	IN FAIRWAY	IN SAND
LW	70 yds.	35 yds.
SW	85 yds.	40 yds.
GW	100 yds.	50 yds.
PW	115 yds.	55 yds.
9-iron	130 yds.	65 yds.
8-iron	145 yds.	75 yds.

How to Beat Ugly Bunkers

Make a 'digging' swing from hard, wet or just plain nasty sand

—Top 100 Teacher Brady Riggs

THIS STORY IS FOR YOU IF...

1
Your don't know how to play shots from hard sand...

2
...except to make ball-first contact.

THE PROBLEM

You've heard that you should open your clubface in a bunker and "float" the ball out on a cushion of sand, but whoever said that has never been to your local muni, where the bunkers look more like wet concrete than soft, sandy cushions.

THE SOLUTION

Your normal bunker shot won't work here because an open face exposes the bounce of your sand wedge, which will carom off the sand and cause you to blade the shot across the green. Instead you'll need to square the clubface and dig it out. Follow these three steps:

1: SET UP LEFT

Lean your weight toward your left side to create a digging angle of attack, and set the face square. The feeling you're after is one of carving the ball out with the lead edge *[photo, below]*, not splashing it out with the sole.

2: DIG IT OUT

Hit just behind the ball and drive the leading edge down into the sand (but don't drive the clubhead so deep that you leave it in the bunker). It should feel like you're chunking a pitch shot from the fairway.

3: FINISH LOW

You're not trying to splash sand here, just to get the leading edge deep enough to pop the ball out. The ball will come out fairly soft, lower and with a little more roll than a normal bunker shot, so plan your landing spot carefully.

Uphill bunker shots come out higher than normal, as long as you swing up the hill.

HOW TO

Blast From a Bunker Upslope

Swing up the hill to get this one on and close

—*Top 100 Teacher Mike LaBauve*

THIS STORY IS FOR YOU IF...

1
You struggle with anything but a flat lie in the bunker.

2
Your tendency here is to jam the club into the hill.

THE SITUATION

Your ball is on the upslope of a bunker. If the pin is close, this lie is an advantage since the ball will fly extra high and land quickly. But if you've hitting to a far pin or into the wind, this becomes a much more difficult shot.

THE SMART PLAY

The key to hitting this shot is to get your body on the same angle as the incline of the bunker by aligning your shoulders with the slope. Most people don't adjust to the lie and either stick the clubhead into the sand, or hit the ball first and fly it over the green.

ON THE NUMBER

Q How close to the hole do PGA Tour pros land greenside bunker shots?

Tour average ☐ Tour leader ☐

Data courtesy PGA Tour ShotLink

PROXIMITY TO THE HOLE FROM GREENSIDE SAND

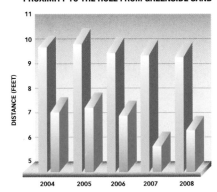

(Bar chart: Y-axis DISTANCE (FEET) from 5 to 11; X-axis years 2004, 2005, 2006, 2007, 2008)

The average Tour player lands bunker shots approximately 5 to 10 feet from the hole every time. They make putts from this distance range at a 52 percent clip.

HOW TO BLAST THE BALL FROM AN UPHILL BUNKER LIE

STEP 1

Use your 56-degree wedge, since the slope will add loft to this shot. With a 60-degree wedge the ball will go straight up and you might leave it in the bunker. Take a wider-than-normal stance, and dig in a little more with your downhill foot for extra support.

STEP 2

You should feel like your shoulders are tilted with the hill. That's' good, because you're going to need to swing up the slope. Make a few practice swings above the ball, getting a feel for moving the clubhead on the same angle as the hill you're standing on.

STEP 3

Because the ball will hit the green and stop with very little roll, you need to take a full swing and make sure the ball can fly all the way to the hole. It's easy to stop your swing at impact because of the slope, so try to hang back on your right side a little longer so your wedge glides through the sand and up the hill.

HOW TO

Blast From a Bunker Downslope

Swing "high-to-low" to beat the toughest bunker lie of them all
—*Top 100 Teacher Mike LaBauve*

THE SITUATION
Your ball has come to rest on a downslope in the bunker.

THE SMART PLAY
Make a "high-to-low" bunker swing (i.e., one that starts at a high position in your backswing and finishes much lower than normal). Follow the steps at right.

THIS STORY IS FOR YOU IF...

1
You hear that this is the most difficult bunker lie...

2
...and your results typically back up this claim.

Continue to swing down the slope even after your club exits the sand.

NOTE:
The downslope takes loft off your club, making it difficult to hit the ball on a high, soft trajectory. As a result, expect the ball to come out lower and with less spin than if you were on a level lie (plan for the extra roll once it hits).

HOW TO BLAST THE BALL FROM A DOWNHILL BUNKER LIE

STEP 1

Like you do on all sloping lies, tilt your shoulders and hips to match the slope. If you do it correctly, your left shoulder will sit below your right shoulder the same amount that your left foot sits below your right foot. Dig your left foot deeper into the sand than your right for extra support.

STEP 2

If you make your normal bunker swing here, your club will hit too far behind the ball, skip off the sand and strike the ball in its equator. You need to swing down the slope. Take a few practice swings over the ball to ingrain the feel of moving the club from a high position in your backswing to a low position in your follow-through.

STEP 3

Enter the sand about an inch behind the ball. Once your club makes contact with the sand, swing down the slope and keep your hands low to the ground all the way into your follow-through. Fight the pull of gravity—it's okay to hang back on your right side on this one so you don't tumble down the hill.

TRY THIS!

The Sit-Down Bunker Shot
It proves just how easy bunker play can be
—*Top 100 Teacher John Elliott Jr.*

No stance, no problem!

During your next practice session, try hitting bunker shots while sitting down, instead of hitting them from your feet. Find a flat portion of the bunker, plop down in the sand, cross your legs and...*just kidding*. There isn't any benefit to practicing sand shots from your rear end. The only lesson is that, yes, it can be done, and fairly easily. I use this trick to start many of my short-game schools, if only to demonstrate how easy bunker play can be. It's not the mysterious voodoo you probably think it is. It's really as simple as "hit the sand and let the sand carry the ball out of the bunker."

Once you get it into your mind that sand shots aren't as difficult as they appear (or as you make them out to be), you'll have an extra bit of confidence every time you step into a bunker, and it will show in your results. Tour players look forward to sand because they know that a play from a bunker is often easier to execute than one from many of the other greenside lies your ball can find when you miss on your approach. Sand swings are a lot easier to make when you trust them.

Blast a Ball Above Your Feet

The trick here is not to take too much sand

—Top 100 Teacher Steve Bosdosh

THIS STORY IS FOR YOU IF...

1
You tend to take too much sand...

2
...which makes sloping lies in the bunker even more difficult.

THE SITUATION

Your approach found the upslope of a greenside bunker. Your lie is good but when you go to take your stance the ball is way above your feet.

THE SOLUTION

With the ball so close to you, the bottom of your natural swing arc occurs too far underneath the ball—you'll take too much sand and likely leave the ball in the bunker. To guard against this, shorten your club by standing tall and choking up on the grip at least two inches. Other than that, make your normal, everyday bunker swing. Follow the steps at right.

TOP 100 TEACHER POLL

Q How much bounce angle do I need on the sole of my sand wedge?

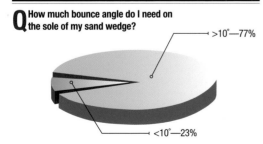

>10°—77%

<10°—23%

"Most golfers assume that extra bounce, like the kinf you'd find on a sand wedge, is helpful only in the sand. But it gives you forgiveness in a lot of other situations." —Top 100 Teacher Jerry Mowlds

STAND TALL
Since the ball is closer to you, stand erect. A straight spine automatically makes your swing flatter—perfect for this situation.

CHEST GAME
To make sure you enter the sand at the right spot and take the right-sized divot, play the ball under the logo of your shirt and aim for a spot in the sand directly under your sternum.

AIM HERE
Like any shot where the ball is above your feet, this one is going to hook left on you. Play the ball right of the flag and let it curl to the cup.

HOW TO BLAST IT FROM SIDEHILL SAND

STEP 1

Copy these setup positions:

1. Choke down on the grip to make the club shorter so you don't dig too deeply into the sand—the common mistake here.

2. Stand erect with your spine nearly straight up and down.

3. Play the ball off the logo of your shirt (just slightly inside your left heel).

4. Dig in with your feet for balance. The more you dig in, the more you should choke up on the club. (Digging in lowers the spot where your swing bottoms out.)

5. Aim right of the hole—this ball wants to go left.

STEP 2

If you make a steep swing [dotted line], you'll bury the club into the hill and the ball will go nowhere. But instead of thinking about making a flatter swing, just take the club back. The reason behind this is that your swing naturally moves around your spine, and if your spine is straight up-and-down, your swing will flatten out by itself.

STEP 3

Copy the picture at left and explode into the sand at a point directly underneath your chest. The explosion will carry the ball out and onto the green. Once the ball hits it will roll left because of the automatic sidespin created by a sidehill lie.

Blasting from a bunker with the ball above your feet requires a unique setup.

Your upright stance causes your swing plane to flatten out. If you trace your normal clubhead path you'll come in too steep.

HOW TO

Blast a Ball Below Your Feet

Your knees are the key to digging the ball out and getting it up and on

—Top 100 Teacher Steve Bosdosh

THIS STORY IS FOR YOU IF...

1
You have a hard time keeping your posture...

2
...which causes you to thin the ball, especially when it's below your feet.

THE SITUATION

You cut your approach shot and found the right-hand side of a bunker on the right side of the green. Not only do you have to stand outside the bunker to take your normal stance, the ball is miles below your feet.

THE SOLUTION

You have a hard time staying down on the ball on regular full swings, so how are you going to do it here? That's a good question to ask your knees, since you'll need to bend them at address in order to get your club down to the ball. More important, they'll have to remain bent during your swing or you'll leave a gash on the top half of the ball. Control your knees and this becomes a relatively simple bunker shot.

FLEX APPEAL
Flex your knees at address and keep them flexed during your swing. As soon as your knees straighten, the odds of you making solid contact plummet.

WIDE STANCE
Standing with your feet wider apart gives you a more solid base from which to swing and drops your club closer to the ball.

HOW TO BLAST THE BALL WHEN IT'S BELOW YOUR FEET

DIG DOWN
Come down sharply into the sand behind the ball. This is a good mental image because the last thing you want is to come in flat. A flat swing when the ball is below your feet will likely result in a skull.

STEP 1 PICK A SPOT
Like any bunker shot, take care when selecting your landing area. (This is a hard shot, but you should still plan to land the ball exactly where you want.) The ball is going to trickle right from this lie, so play left of the pin.

STEP 2 HUNKER DOWN
Set the ball off the logo of your shirt and then…

1 Take a wider stance.

2 Bend from your hips until your back is nearly parallel to the ground.

3 Flex your knees.

These setup moves position the bottom of your swing arc below the ball.

STEP 3 GET STEEP
With a flat spine your swing automatically gets steep, so you don't have to think about moving the club way above plane—just take it back and through like a normal sand shot.

"The secret is to lower the bottom of your swing arc by adjusting your stance, not your swing."

Beat a Buried Lie

No more Mr. Nice Guy! Give this bad lie the beating it deserves.

—*Top 100 Teacher Jon Tattersall*

THIS STORY IS FOR YOU IF...

1
Your course features bunkers with soft, fluffy sand.

2
You're more of a picker than a blaster.

THE SITUATION

Your approach landed in a greenside bunker. When you step into the bunker, you can only see the top half of the ball. Your first thought is, "Can I deem this an unplayable lie?"

THE SMART PLAY

Buried lies like this are no picnic. Your only hope is to dig the ball out and hope it lands somewhere close. The secret is to turn your sand wedge from a splashing tool into a digging tool. Step one: Set the leading edge of your wedge square to your target and get ready for the biggest bunker swing you can make. Since this lie requires extra muscle power, take a wider stance than normal. This lowers your center of gravity and gives you an extra dose of stability as you try to dig down underneath the ball and pop it up and onto the green.

Pound the sand behind and underneath the ball to get it up and on the green from a buried lie.

Take an extra-wide stance to support what's going to be an extra-big swing, and set the leading edge of your wedge square to your target line.

HOW TO BLAST A BALL ON FROM A BURIED LIE

1 Set up with your nose over the ball and your feet spread wide for extra stability when you swing.

2 Swing the club back normally, making sure to extend your arms while also hinging your wrists.

3 Think of this swing as a power swing that you make around a stable head and lower body.

4 You don't need to take the club all the way back. It's more important that you hinge your wrists fully.

5 Lead your downswing with your lower body. Your extra-wide stance gives you all the stability you'll need.

6 Keep the flex in your knees. Notice that my weight has moved forward, but not my head.

7 Feel your right arm extending down into impact. You'll need this extension to dig the ball out.

8 At impact, your left arm and the shaft should line up. Save some hinge in your right wrist to power the club down.

9 Notice how the sand slows down my swing, but how I maintain pressure from the club into the sand.

10 Evidence of a proper digging action is that both arms are straight with the hands still leading the clubhead.

11 Not a hint of a picking action—you need to take a lot of sand to get this one out. That's your goal.

12 Knees are still flexed, meaning every ounce of energy in your swing went into the sand.

Add an extra dose of creativity—and the Top 100 Teachers' bag of trick shots—to make easy work of any tough situation around the green.

8

SHORT GAME SHORT CUTS

When run-of-the-mill techniques won't do, turn to these score-saving short-game supershots

CREATIVE WAYS TO SAVE PAR

Good short-game players can seemingly pull a rabbit out of their hat on command, turning sure-bogey situations into miraculous pars saves and, at times, eye-popping birdies. While it's difficult to find time to practice specialty shots and trick swings, especially when you consider the work that's required to keep your full-swing fundamentals in good shape, adding a dose of creativity to your game never goes out of style, and is usually what separates the best players from everybody else. If you don't know where to start, add the following short-game plays to your shotmaking arsenal and see where they take you. Not only will they keep your scores from ballooning when you face tough situations around the green, they'll open up your creative mind to a never-ending list of tricky, yet trustworthy, shot options.

Hit Five Perfect Short Shots

This simple shot arsenal will get you close from a majority of greenside lies

—Top 100 Teacher Bill Forrest

THE SITUATION

You're 30 yards from the green and need to get up and down to stay in your match. You've been in this situation many times before, and you've almost always pulled the wrong club or hit the wrong kind of shot.

THE SMART PLAY

A simple, easy-to-remember repertoire of shots would help, and here's how to get it. All you need to store in your memory bank are two setups and three swings, then pull them up on the course to generate five different trajectories with specific amounts of carry and roll.

THE SETUPS

70%

55%

A: CHIP ADDRESS

Play the ball back in your stance and set your hands in front of your zipper. The shaft should lean toward the target. Set approximately 70 percent of your weight on your left foot, and keep it there.

B: PITCH ADDRESS

Play the ball in the middle of your stance. The shaft should sit nearly vertical to the ground. Set approximately 55 percent of your weight on your left foot, and keep it there during your swing.

SHOT 5
LOFTED PITCH
Use it: When you have to carry an obstacle, or there's little green to land the ball between the fringe and the flagstick.

SHOT 4
STANDARD PITCH
Use it: When you need to carry the ball onto the green or just short of it, and then make it check so it doesn't roll past the hole.

SHOT 1
LOW RUNNING CHIP
Use it: When you have lots of green to work with, or are playing to an elevated tier.

SHOT 2
STANDARD CHIP
Use it: When you have less green to work with, and there aren't any obstacles between you and the green.

HOW TO HIT EACH SHOT

Combine the right club with one of the two setups *[below left]* and one of the three swings *[right]* to snuggle the ball close from any lie.

SWING	1	2	3	4	5
Carry:Roll (%)	25:75	40:60	60:40	75:25	90:10
Club	7-iron	PW	LW	LW	LW
Setup	A	A	B	B	B
Swing	1	1	1	2	3

Before attempting these shots, stand behind the ball and draw a picture in your mind of the trajectory that would work best for the situation you're facing. See the ball carry in the air and roll out to the cup once it hits the ground. Get a real sense of the perfect shot shape, then select one of the five shots discussed here that best match the carry and roll values you pictured in your mind.

SHOT 3
LOFTED CHIP
Use it: When you need to loft the ball onto the green, but you still want it to run once it hits.

THE SWINGS

#1: NONE-NONE
(No-hinge backswing, No-hinge through-swing)

Use this for each of the low chip shots. Make more of a putting stroke than a chip stroke using the same pace both back and through. Hold your wrists firm on both sides of the ball, and keep your hands below your belt line.

#2: SOME-NONE
(Medium-hinge backswing, No-hinge through-swing)

Use this swing for the standard pitch (#4). Unlike the swing you use when hitting the three chip shots, hinge your wrists on your backswing, and unhinge them coming back down. This hinging action is what gives your shot height so you can carry the ball farther and control the roll once it lands on the green. Once you make impact, keep your wrists firm and finish low to the ground.

#3: MORE-MORE
(Full-hinge backswing, Full-hinge through-swing)

To generate maximum carry with little roll you need to hinge your wrists on both sides of the ball. This kind of wrist action puts maximum loft on the shot, allowing you to carry the ball almost the full distance to the pin. It's the same swing you'd use to hit an explosion shot in a bunker.

HOW TO

Hit A Bank-Shot Chip

Save par when you don't have enough green to land even a flop shot

—*Top 100 Teacher Shawn Humphries*

THIS STORY IS FOR YOU IF...

1
Your course features collection areas around the green.

2
You fear the flop shot.

WHAT IT IS
A hard chip shot hit into the bank of a hill. The ball shoots straight up after it strikes the slope and lands like a butterfly with sore feet on the green.

WHEN TO USE IT
You've missed a crowned green to the left or right and settled into a collection area. There's a slope in front of you and, worse yet, very little green between the fringe and the pin. There's not even enough green to hold a high-lofted shot.

HOW TO HIT IT
The most important weapon in your short game is your imagination, and you need to use it here. Instead of attempting an impossible flop or skating a chip across the green, bump the ball into the slope in front of you. Follow the steps below.

FORM A LINE
Restrict your follow-through and keep the club in-line with your hands.

FEET TOGETHER
Play this shot with your feet close together and your weight leaning slightly to the left.

HOW TO BANK THE BALL CLOSE

STEP 1
Find your target on the bank. Generally, it will be a spot about three-quarters of the way up the hill. (Make sure the bank is steep enough so that the force of the ball will cause it to bounce up and not skip forward.)

STEP 2
Set up with your feet close together, your hands pressed forward and your weight favoring your left side. Play the ball just a shade back of center, since the last thing you want to do here is hit up on the ball (you'll add loft and miss the bank completely).

STEP 3
Make an extremely aggressive chip swing without any release and with a limited follow-through *[photo, above]*. Notice how the hands are still in line with the club and how the club hasn't released.

DANGER!
Miss the hill and you may never see your ball again. Err on using too little loft rather than too much loft when playing this shot.

...and end up next to the hole.

...watch it pop up to here...

Hit it here...

Play a bank shot from deep collection areas.

Although this is a short shot, don't treat it like a chip. In fact, your swing should feel long and smooth—like the one you'd use out of a bunker. Follow through to about a three-quarter finish.

HOW TO

Super-Size Your Flop

Cup your left wrist to loft the ball high and stop it in its tracks
—*Top 100 Teacher Mike Davis*

THE SITUATION

You've short-sided yourself and need to carry a bunker or water hazard without much room to land the ball. This isn't the time for your run-of-the-mill lob. Follow the steps on this page to get extra height and stopping power to flop this ball tight.

STEP 1

Grab your lob wedge and set up with the ball positioned between the center of your stance and your left foot, and tilt the shaft away from the target. This aggressive shaft lean adds loft to your club without requiring you to open the face, which reduces the available strike area and makes for a more difficult shot.

STEP 2

Notice that when you lean the shaft back your left wrist cups, or bends backward. That's the secret ingredient to this shot. Maintain the cup from start through impact and into your follow-through. It's important to keep the handle behind the ball at impact. This allows the sole of your club to skip under the ball.

HOW TO

Stick Slick Downhill Chips

This right-foot trick stops you from blading the ball across the green

—*Top 100 Teacher Eden Foster*

THE SITUATION

Your approach shot missed the green and stopped on the side of a hill. You're now looking at one of the toughest short-game shots around: the downhill chip.

THE SMART PLAY

Notice that when you take your stance you get the feeling that the ball will come out too low. Most golfers compensate for this by hanging back on their right foot and scooping the ball into the air, which almost always leads to a skull. The secret to avoiding this mistake is to totally remove your right foot from the equation and plan for a lower shot. The ball will come out more like a 9-iron than a lob wedge, but with practice you'll learn to get this shot close to the hole.

THIS STORY IS FOR YOU IF...

1
Downhill chips terrify you because you usually skull the ball.

2
You don't think you can hit the ball high or soft enough from a downhill lie.

STEP 3
Feel like you're moving the club up the hill going back and then down the hill coming through—you should finish low and with little follow-through. Basically, you're trying to trace the hill with your clubhead.

...swing with the slope.

Lift your right foot...

...weaken your grip...

STEP 1
Grab your highest-lofted club, take your normal address and lift your right heel, which will keep you from hanging back on your right side. Align your shoulders to the slope.

STEP 2
Weaken your grip—your right hand should feel like it's on top of your left hand. This will prevent you from releasing the club (and delofting it).

HOW TO

Chip It Closer with Your Putter

A wristy stroke with your trusty flatstick takes the fear out of delicate short shots

—*Top 100 Teacher Carol Preisinger*

THIS STORY IS FOR YOU IF...

1
You're not comfortable chipping from tight lies.

2
Your course features smoothly cut aprons and fringe.

THE SITUATION

You landed short of the green in a collection area. The pin is cut toward the front of the green, leaving you with little room to land the ball between the fringe and the cup. You'd normally hit a soft chip from this situation, but the tightly mown grass makes you think twice—you're prone to blading the ball from tight lies.

THE SMART PLAY

As long as you're within 10 yards of the green, hit the shot with your putter. It's usually the club you hit straightest and with which you make the best contact—a good recipe for the shot at hand. You won't have to worry about the ball coming up short of the green since the grass is so tightly cut. Plus, you're going to add a new wrinkle to your stroke to get the ball smoothly rolling off the face of your putter with ample speed.

Use your flatstick when the lie is so tight you fear catching the shot thin with your wedge.

STEP 1
Set up like you're hitting a short chip. Play the ball a little further forward in your stance to make sure you catch the ball on a slight upswing.

STEP 2
Swing your hands back just a foot or so while gently hinging the club up with your wrists. As you do this, keep the putterface pointing at the ball.

STEP 3
Swing your hands forward while releasing the hinge you built into your wrists on your backswing. Your wrist action gives the shot enough pop to roll the ball across the grass, across the apron and onto the green.

Pick the Right Club

It's one easy step to discover the wedge that gives you the trajectory you need for the shot at hand

—Top 100 Teacher Shawn Humphries

When you step on the clubface until it's parallel with the ground, the shaft will show you the club's trajectory.

THIS STORY IS FOR YOU IF...

1
You don't know the trajectory of shots with each club.

2
You chip with the same club every time (a bad idea).

THE PROBLEM

You know to use a more lofted club if you want to hit a chip shot that carries more in the air, and a lower-lofted club to get the ball rolling earlier, but the key to being a good chipper is to know which trajectory will give you the proper amount of carry and roll to reach the hole for a given situation.

THE SOLUTION

Here's an easy way to figure out the trajectory of a chip with any club. Lay the club along the ground with the clubface up and the shaft pointing toward your target. Now step down on the clubface until the back of the club is flat against the ground. The angle that the shaft rises to is the trajectory of the shots you'll produce with that club.

TOP 100 TEACHER POLL

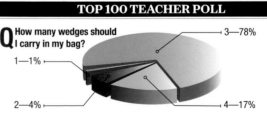

Q How many wedges should I carry in my bag?

- 3—78%
- 1—1%
- 2—4%
- 4—17%

"My research on the short game near the end of the last decade concluded that golfers required even more loft to stop the ball quickly. In addition to your gap, sand and lob wedges, add a 64-degree wedge. More than 40 players on Tour now carry four wedges."—Top 100 Teacher Dave Pelz

LEARN THE

Easy Way to Run It Up Close

Try this savvy play when you have a clear shot to the flagstick

—Top 100 Teacher Scott Munroe

THIS STORY IS FOR YOU IF...

1
You know it's a good idea to get the ball rolling on the ground as soon as possible...

2
...but don't know how to keep it low without hitting the shot thin.

THE SITUATION

You've come up a good 20 yards short of the green. Your path is hazard-free, and there's plenty of green to work with.

THE SMART PLAY

Make an easy chip swing with any of your wedges using any of the techniques in this book.

THE SMARTER PLAY

Unless you've built a trustworthy repertoire of short swings that generate specific distances and specific amounts of carry and roll, hitting the ball close from 20-30 yards is an iffy proposition. That's when a shot like the hinge-and-drop hybrid can help. It's an elementary swing that takes guesswork out of the equation and rolls the ball 25 yards on the number every time. Follow the steps at right.

HOW TO DO IT

STEP 1
Grab your most-lofted hybrid, grip down on the middle of the handle, set your feet together and position the ball just outside your right foot. Move your hands in front of your zipper so that the shaft leans toward the target.

STEP 2
Without moving your arms, hinge the club up with your wrists as far as your joints will allow. Make sure you hinge without cupping your left wrists. If your left wrist cups, the clubface will fly open.

STEP 3
Using your wrists only, hinge the club down into the back of the ball. Do it smoothly, and stop your swing at contact. The ball will pop up and run out 25 to 30 yards almost every time.

Pop It On From the Rough

This crafty putt-chip frees you from the junk and gets you to tap-in range

—*Top 100 Teacher Martin Hall*

THIS STORY IS FOR YOU IF...

1
The greens at your course are encircled by pretty nasty rough.

2
You often flub chip shots from long grass.

THE SITUATION

You missed on your approach—barely. The ball sits just off the green, but unfortunately in some pretty hairy rough. You're not sure you can make a clean strike with your wedge, unless you really power it through the junk. If you do, however, the ball will go too far.

THE SMART PLAY

Getting a wedge through rough isn't easy, especially when you're facing short distances around the green. The trick is to realize that you only need to pop the ball out of the rough and let the roll do the rest. There are dozens of ways to accomplish this task, but one is easier than all the rest: pop it out with your putter. Your flatstick is the shortest club in your bag, meaning it's the easiest to control. Plus, it gives you the widest strike area—a good asset when you're swinging though long grass.

STEP 1
Take your normal putting stance, but position the ball just outside your right foot. Set your hands in front of your zipper so that the shaft leans toward the target.

STEP 2
Smoothly hinge the club up with your wrists without moving your arms. This is all the backswing you need.

STEP 3
Release the hinge in your wrists and bring the putterhead into the back of the ball on a descending path. You'll know you did it correctly if the ball pops up before it starts moving forward.

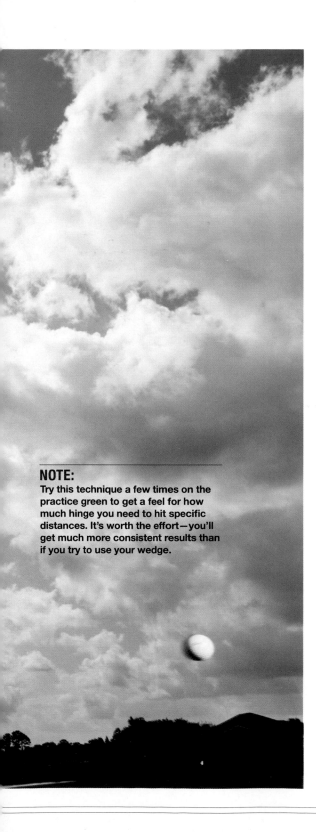

NOTE:
Try this technique a few times on the practice green to get a feel for how much hinge you need to hit specific distances. It's worth the effort—you'll get much more consistent results than if you try to use your wedge.

HOW TO

Escape Bunkers Without Thinking

The often-overlooked art of "digging in" gives you a perfect bunker swing almost automatically

—*Top 100 Teacher Mark Hackett*

THIS STORY IS FOR YOU IF...

1
You're a suspect bunker player at best.

2
You never dig your feet into the sand when you play shots from bunkers.

CHECK THIS!

Step into any practice bunker, take your address and swing. If you're like most golfers, you forgot a very important step: digging in with your feet. Sure, you shuffled your feet to get comfortable in the sand, but you likely didn't dig those puppies deep into the sand.

WHY IT'S IMPORTANT

The more you dig your feet into the sand, the more you lower the bottom of your swing arc below the surface of the bunker. This allows you to enter the sand behind the ball, swing directly underneath the ball, and exit the sand in front of the ball without worrying about how to manipulate your wedge to make it all happen. Once you're dug in, all you need to do is swing. You'll take the perfect sand divot every time.

Dig your feet deep into the sand to lower your swing arc and take the perfect-sized sand divot without thinking about your swing.

Chip It Out of a Bunker

Forget the blast. Make a safer—and easier—play on long bunker shots
—*Top 100 Teacher Shawn Humphries*

THIS STORY IS FOR YOU IF...

1
You come up short on longer bunker shots.

2
Your club often gets stuck in the sand.

THE SITUATION

You're stuck in a greenside bunker, about 50 feet from the hole. This is a tough shot even for Tour players.

THE SOLUTION

Instead of hitting a long bunker blast (one of the toughest shots you can try), chip the ball out of the bunker. A chip is easier to control once it hits the green and allows you to manage your mis-hits. Even if you leave it short, you'll guarantee bogey. Plus, you don't have to worry about making a big swing and taking the right amount of sand.

HOW TO CHIP IT FROM A BUNKER

STEP 1
Take a short iron (7-, 8- or 9-iron, depending on distance) and choke down midway on the grip. Set up with your feet close together and your body leaning forward. Keep everything square to your intended line. Your sternum should be a little in front of the ball and your hands should be pressed forward.

HOW TO PRACTICE IT
Practice this shot by drawing a line in the sand and chip balls off it. Your divot should show the club entering the sand at the back of the line and taking a divot in front of the line [photo, below]. This isn't an explosion shot, but you should comb the sand enough to take a bit of it out of the bunker.

Target

Stay firm with your left side. Don't break down and try to scoop the ball.

STEP 2
Use your regular chipping technique and make a crisp pop on the ball. Try to catch the ball a little before the sand. You'll need more swing speed than your normal chip because the ground breaks away beneath the ball in a bunker and you need to roll it 40-50 feet.

NOTE:
If the bunker you're in isn't very steep and your lie is good, bust the ball out using your basic chipping stroke.

IMPORTANT:
On normal sand shots you want to hit behind the ball. When you chip it out of the sand, you want your divot to be on the target side of the ball.

Get Long Chip Shots Close

It's easy—use hybrid power!

—*Top 100 Teacher Martin Hall*

THE SITUATION

You landed a few yards short of the green on your approach. The lie isn't bad, but the flag is all the way on the other side of the green.

THE SMART PLAY

Hopefully, by now, you've learned that you have the best chance of getting the ball close if you get it rolling on the ground as soon as possible. That seems like a strange play here since you have so much green to work with, but trust me—rolling the ball the right distance is easier than flying the ball the right distance.

If you're like most golfers, however, you have difficulty getting the ball on the ground with your wedges. Understandable—these are the most lofted clubs in your bag. So opt for something with a little less loft and a longer shaft so that you can make a small swing and generate enough distance to traverse the green. Play a slow roller with your hybrid.

HOW TO ROLL IT TIGHT WITH YOUR HYBRID

STEP 1
Use your chipping setup, gripping down on the handle of your most-lofted hybrid so that it fits your stance.

Roll the ball to the hole even when you have lots of green to work with.

STEP 2
Place your hands on the sides of the grip so that your palms face each other. Anchor your right hand to the grip by laying your left index finger over the fingers of your right hand. This grip makes it difficult for the club to pass your hands on your downswing.

STEP 3
Although you're set up to chip, make more of a putting backstroke, using mostly your arms. Try to keep the face of your hybrid pointing at your target.

STEP 4
Bring the club back to the ball with your upper body by turning your torso toward the target. Feel like your elbows are pinned to the sides of your torso so that your arms swing forward with the turning motion of your upper body. This gives you a nice, controlled strike. The ball will pop off the face softly and start rolling end-over-end immediately. The biggest mistake you can make is to let the clubhead pass your hands on your through-swing. That's when you'll catch it thin.

Play Short Shots without a Backswing

Make chips, pitches—even putts— easy by eliminating the source of 70 percent of your errors: your backswing

—Top 100 Teacher Dr. T.J. Tomasi

THIS STORY IS FOR YOU IF...

1
Every facet of your short game needs help.

2
You aren't sure where you're making mistakes in your swing.

THE SITUATION

If you're like most golfers, you understand intuitively that most of your swing errors start in your backswing. You're right—70 percent of all full-swing mistakes can be traced to your backswing. That's the reason my colleague, Dr. Jim Suttie, and I developed the No-Backswing Swing, the mechanics of which were published in the September 2007 issue of *GOLF Magazine*. Since that time we've discovered that the principles of the No-Backswing Swing are even more effective for your short-game shots. The No-Backswing Swing, or NBS, works because it allows you to dial in all of the necessary parameters before you start your downswing. This way, you have only a quarter of a second to make a mistake—usually not enough time for disaster, even for the most error-prone players.

THE BOTTOM LINE

The major advantage of the No-Backswing Short Game is that if you aim the clubface correctly at address, it will look down your intended line at impact. This is the key to good shots, because the ball is going to take on the characteristics of the clubface at impact. Since the majority of errors happen during the backswing, you eliminate the errors when you eliminate the backswing. It's true for your full-swings, your pitches, your chips and your putts.

Compared to oddities like the belly putter, the No-Backswing Short Game looks practically normal.

HOW TO PLAY THE NO-BACKSWING CHIP

Here's a good rule of thumb: If you're within six paces of the green, chip the ball. And if you're going to chip the ball, why not eliminate your backswing? This simplifies the chipping motion, reducing the clutter in your mind and allowing you to isolate and perfect your downswing and impact positions.

STEP 1: SET THE CLUB

Set up with your feet and hips open to the target line while your shoulders stay square. The ball should be back in your stance, and your weight should be on your left foot. Based on how far you want this shot to travel, determine the length of your backswing and move the club back to 95 percent of that length.

Low hands, low club.

STEP 2: DO THE PUMP

Once you're set at 95 percent of your backswing length, make sure the clubhead is square to the path. Then make a slight pump with your shoulders so the clubhead moves about 5 percent more away from the target. This will give you some rhythm—it's similar to how a baseball player cocks his bat before he swings.

STEP 3: KEEP IT LOW

Your goal is to move the club back through the ball with a constant rotation of your core area—imagine an eight-inch box on your torso with your navel in the center. You should finish with approximately the same length of swing on the other side of impact—without any wrist break. Your stroke should be low to the ground and much like a putt. Think low hands, low clubhead.

Rotating my core allows my hands to be quiet through impact, reducing sidespin and increasing accuracy.

HOW TO PLAY THE NO-BACKSWING PITCH

Think of your pitch shot as your air route to the flag. If you're more than six paces from the green and there's trouble like rough or a hazard between you and the green, you should pitch the ball. Here's how to control your pitches more easily with the No-Backswing Swing technique.

STEP 1: SET THE CLUB

Set up with your feet, hips and shoulders open to the target line and your clubface aimed at the target. The ball should be slightly forward. Determine the length of your backswing and set the club at 95 percent of it. Swing your arms back along your foot line and set your wrists so that the clubhead is high and your hands are low.

Low hands, high clubhead.

STEP 2: DO THE PUMP

Check the clubface to make sure it's open to the target line the amount you desire. Then make a slight pump with your shoulders so the clubhead moves about 5 percent farther away from the target. This will give your pitching swing some rhythm, just as it did for the chip shot.

STEP 3: DON'T LIFT

Swing the club through the ball along your foot line—not along your target line, which causes a shank. Move the club with a constant rotation of your core and don't try to lift the ball up or drop your back shoulder to get under the ball—you want to hit the back of the ball, not under it.

STEP 4: KEEP QUIET

Finish with roughly the same length of swing on the other side of impact—your wrists should have re-cocked to match the pose at the top of your backswing. The No-Backswing Swing is a quiet one—all you do is rotate your core and keep moving.

The NBS pitch allows you to create a straight line from your right shoulder to the clubface, which keeps the face from shutting down.

BONUS LESSON: HOW TO PLAY THE NO-BACKSWING PUTT

The putting equation is simple: Good Distance + Good Direction = Good Putting. The NBS obviously helps your aim—no more off-line backswings— but it also helps your distance. Each player has an "applied force fingerprint"—a combination of force and swing length. For example, David Toms has a long back-and-through stroke with a soft force application, while Tiger Woods is shorter on both sides but applies more force. With the NBS you can quickly identify your fingerprint, because when you eliminate errors your application of force becomes more consistent.

STEP 1: SET THE CLUB
It makes no difference if you are an inside-to-square putter or a straight-back, straight-through advocate. Just set your putterface on the path you want and check it. Note how low I've set the putterhead here—this is the key to returning the putter to its "true loft" at impact.

STEP 2: DO THE PUMP
Make a slight pump with your shoulders so that the clubhead moves about 5 percent farther away from your target. The pump is to give your putting stroke rhythm, and your goal should be to not disrupt your preset face or path during the pump.

STEP 3: KEEP IT LEVEL
Note that the putter-head is very low to the ground to assure a level face at impact. Too often players allow the putterhead to lift too high off the ground in their backswings and return too steeply, which causes skidding and bouncing.

In the NBS stroke, the hands are clamps— they don't move the putter, they anchor it.

QUIZ TIME
Is the NBS Short Game Right For You?

Do you alternate between hitting your pitches fat and thin, with fat predominating?
NO: Skip to the next question
YES: Switch to the NBS

If you commonly chunk your chips, you're using your hands to move the clubhead. With the NBS your hands are pre-cocked so you can rotate with just enough chest turn back and through to move the clubhead and avoid excess use of your hands.

Do your chip shots often stop way short and other times run too far past?
NO: Skip to the next question
YES: Switch to the NBS

Chances are you're applying too much spin to your chips by striking them with an open face. Spin is good only if you plan for it. If you're not planning for it, then spin is the enemy of roll. With the NBS, you set the amount of face angle you want for the chip (open, closed, square) at the top and then simply keep the face moving through impact.

Do you have trouble setting the club at the top of your swing?
NO: Keep your regular swing, but you can use the NBS for practice
YES: Switch to the NBS

All of the Tour players I tested adapted to the NBS easily because they didn't overuse their hands for pitching and chipping. They knew how to hit it with their core rotation. Most amateurs are too handsy with their short-game shots, and the NBS is a great way to learn what moves the clubhead. It's core, not hands.

THE TOP 100 TEACHERS IN AMERICA

A quick look at the nation's most exclusive—and talented—team of teaching experts

MIKE ADAMS
Facility: Hamilton Farms G.C., Gladstone, N.J.
Website: www.mikeadamsgolf.com
Teaching since: 1977
Top 100 since: 1996

ROB AKINS
Facility: Ridgeway C.C., Germantown, Tenn.
Website: www.robakinsgolf.com
Teaching since: 1987
Top 100 since: 2001

ERIC ALPENFELS
Facility: The Pinehurst G.A., Pinehurst, N.C.
Website: www.pinehurst.com
Teaching since: 1984
Top 100 since: 2001

TODD ANDERSON
Facility: Sea Island Golf Learning Center, St. Simons Island, Ga.
Website: www.seaisland.com
Teaching since: 1984
Top 100 since: 2003

ROBERT BAKER
Facility: Logical Golf, Miami Beach, Fla.
Website: www.logicalgolf.com
Teaching since: 1989
Top 100 since: 1999

RICK BARRY
Facility: Sea Pines Resort, Hilton Head Island, S.C.
Website: www.seapines.com
Teaching since: 1976
Top 100 since: 2005

MIKE BENDER
Facility: Mike Bender Golf Academy at Timacuan C.C., Lake Mary, Fla.
Website: www.mikebender.com
Teaching since: 1990
Top 100 since: 1996

STEVE BOSDOSH
Facility: Members Club at Four Streams, Beallsville, Md.
Website: www.fourstreams.com
Teaching since: 1983
Top 100 since: 2001

MICHAEL BREED
Facility: Sunningdale C.C., Scarsdale, N.Y.
Website: www.michaelbreed.com
Teaching since: 1986
Top 100 since: 2003

BRAD BREWER
Facility: Brad Brewer Golf Academy at Shingle Creek Resort, Orlando, Fla.
Website: www.bradbrewer.com
Teaching since: 1984
Top 100 since: 2007

ANNE CAIN
Facility: Anne Cain Golf Academy, Amelia Island, Fla.
Website: www.annecaingolf.com
Teaching since: 1995
Top 100 since: 2007

JASON CARBONE
Facility: Jim McLean G.S., Litchfield Park, Ariz.
Website: www.jimmclean.com/usa/wigwam
Teaching since: 1993
Top 100 since: 2007

DONALD CRAWLEY
Facility: The Boulders Golf Academy, Carefree, Ariz.
Website: www.golfsimplified.com
Teaching since: 1974
Top 100 since: 1999

JOHN DAHL
Facility: Oxbow C.C., Oxbow, N.D.
Website: www.oxbowcc.com
Teaching since: 1974
Top 100 since: 2003

BILL DAVIS
Facility: Jupiter Hills Club, Tequesta, Fla.
Website: www.jupiterhillsclub.org
Teaching since: 1973
Top 100 since: 1996

MIKE DAVIS
Facility: Walters Golf Academy, Las Vegas, Nev.
Website: www.waltersgolf.com
Teaching since: 1970
Top 100 since: 2007

GLENN DECK
Facility: Pelican Hill Golf Academy, Newport Coast, Calif.
Website: www.pelicanhill.com
Teaching since: 1983
Top 100 since: 2003

DOM DIJULIA
Facility: Dom DiJulia School of Golf, New Hope, Pa.
Website: www.dijuliagolf.com
Teaching since: 1990
Top 100 since: 2007

JOHN ELLIOTT, JR.
Facility: Golden Ocala Golf & Equestrian Club, Ocala, Fla.
Website: www.goldenocala.com
Teaching since: 1970
Top 100 since: 1996

CHUCK EVANS
Facility: Emerald Bay Golf Club, Destin, Fla.
Website: www.medicusgolfinstitute.com
Teaching since: 1970
Top 100 since: 2009

BILL FORREST
Facility: Troon Country Club, Scottsdale, Ariz.
Website: www.trooncc.com
Teaching since: 1978
Top 100 since: 2007

EDEN FOSTER
Facility: Maidstone Club, East Hampton, N.Y.
Website: www.maidstoneclub.com
Teaching since: 1988
Top 100 since: 2003

JANE FROST
Facility: Jane Frost Golf School at Sandwich Hollows G.C., Sandwich, Mass.
Website: www.janefrostgolfschools.com
Teaching since: 1982
Top 100 since: 1996

BRYAN GATHRIGHT
Facility: Oak Hills C.C., San Antonio, Tex.
Website: www.oakhillscc.com
Teaching since: 1987
Top 100 since: 2001

DAVID GLENZ

Facility: David Glenz Golf Academy, Franklin, N.J.
Website: www.davidglenz.com
Teaching since: 1978
Top 100 since: 1996

PATRICK GOSS

Facility: Northwestern University, Evanston, Ill.
Website: www.northwestern.edu/athletics
Teaching since: 1993
Top 100 since: 2007

RICK GRAYSON

Facility: Connie Morris Golf Learning Center, Springfield, Mo.
Website: www.rickgraysongolf.com
Teaching since: 1976
Top 100 since: 1996

FRED GRIFFIN

Facility: Grand Cypress Academy of Golf, Orlando, Fla.
Website: www.grandcypress.com
Teaching since: 1980
Top 100 since: 1996

RON GRING

Facility: Gring Golf, Daphne, Ala.
Website: www.gringgolf.com
Teaching since: 1977
Top 100 since: 2003

ROGER GUNN

Facility: Tierra Rejada G.C., Moorpark, Calif.
Website: www.golflevels.com
Teaching since: 1993
Top 100 since: 2007

MARK HACKETT

Facility: Old Palm G.C., Palm Beach Gardens, Fla.
Teaching since: 1988
Top 100 since: 2009

MARTIN HALL

Facility: Ibis Golf & C.C., West Palm Beach, Fla.
Website: www.ibisgolf.com
Teaching since: 1978
Top 100 since: 1996

HANK HANEY

Facility: Hank Haney Golf Ranch, McKinney, Tex.
Website: www.hankhaney.com
Teaching since: 1977
Top 100 since: 1996

JIM HARDY

Facility: Jacobsen/Hardy Golf, Houston, Tex.
Website: www.jimhardygolf.com
Teaching since: 1966
Top 100 since: 1996

BUTCH HARMON, JR.

Facility: Butch Harmon School of Golf, Henderson, Nev..
Website: www.butchharmon.com
Teaching since: 1965
Top 100 since: 1996

CRAIG HARMON

Facility: Oak Hill C.C., Rochester, N.Y.
Website: www.oakhillcc.com
Teaching since: 1968
Top 100 since: 1996

SHAWN HUMPHRIES

Facility: Cowboys G.C., Grapevine, Tex.
Website: www.shawnhumphries.com
Teaching since: 1988
Top 100 since: 2005

DON HURTER

Facility: Castle Pines G.C., Castle Rock, Colo.
Website: None
Teaching since: 1987
Top 100 since: 2003

ED IBARGUEN

Facility: Duke University G.C., Durham, N.C.
Website: www.golf.duke.edu
Teaching since: 1979
Top 100 since: 2001

HANK JOHNSON

Facility: Greystone G.C., Birmingham, Ala.
Website: www.greystonecc.com
Teaching since: 1969
Top 100 since: 1999

CHARLIE KING

Facility: Reynolds Plantation, Greensboro, Ga.
Website: www.reynoldsgolfacademy.com
Teaching since: 1989
Top 100 since: 2003

JERRY KING

Facility: Kapalua Golf Academy, Lahaina, Maui, Hi.
Website: www.jerrykinggolf.com
Teaching since: 1992
Top 100 since: 2009

PETER KOSTIS

Facility: Kostis/McCord Learning Center, Scottsdale, AZ
Website: www.kostismccordlearning.com
Teaching since: 1971
Top 100 since: 1996

DON KOTNIK

Facility: Toledo Country Club, Toledo, Ohio
Website: www.toledocountryclub.com
Teaching since: 1969
Top 100 since: 2005

PETER KRAUSE

Facility: Hank Haney International Junior Golf Academy, Hilton Head, S.C.
Website: www.peterkrausegolf.com
Teaching since: 1981
Top 100 since: 1999

MIKE LaBAUVE

Facility: Westin Kierland Resort and Spa, Scottsdale, Ariz.
Website: www.kierlandresort.com
Teaching since: 1980
Top 100 since: 1996

SANDY LaBAUVE

Facility: Westin Kierland Resort and Spa, Scottsdale, Ariz.
Website: www.kierlandresort.com
Teaching since: 1984
Top 100 since: 1996

ROD LIDENBERG

Facility: Prestwick G.C., Woodbury, Minn.
Website: www.pgamasterpro.com
Teaching since: 1972
Top 100 since: 2007

MICHAEL LOPUSZYNSKI

Facility: David Glenz G.A., Franklin, N.J.
Website: www.davidglenz.com
Teaching since: 1987
Top 100 since: 1996

JACK LUMPKIN

Facility: Sea Island Golf Learning Center, St. Simons Island, Ga.
Website: www.seaisland.com
Teaching since: 1958
Top 100 since: 1996

KEITH LYFORD

Facility: Golf Academy at Old Greenwood, Truckee, Calif.
Website: www.lyfordgolf.net
Teaching since: 1982
Top 100 since: 1999

BILL MADONNA

Facility: Bill Madonna G.A, Orlando, Fla.
Website: www.marriottworldcenter.com
Teaching since: 1971
Top 100 since: 1996

TIM MAHONEY

Facility: Talking Stick G.C., Scottsdale, Ariz.
Website: www.timmahoneygolf.com
Teaching since: 1980
Top 100 since: 1996

MIKE MALASKA

Facility: Superstition Mountain G. & C.C., Superstition Mountain, Ariz.
Website: www.malaskagolf.com
Teaching since: 1982
Top 100 since: 1996

PAUL MARCHAND
Facility: Shadow Hawk G.C., Richmond, Tex.
Website: www.golfspan.com
Teaching since: 1981
Top 100 since: 1996

LYNN MARRIOTT
Facility: Vision 54, Phoenix, Ariz.
Website: www.vision54.com
Teaching since: 1982
Top 100 since: 1996

RICK MARTINO
Facility: Motion Golf, Palm Beach Gardens, Fla.
Website: www.motiongolf.com
Teaching since: 1970
Top 100 since: 2003

RICK McCORD
Facility: McCord Golf Academy at Orange Lake Resort, Kissimmee, Fla.
Website: www.themccordgolfacademy.com
Teaching since: 1973
Top 100 since: 1996

GERALD McCULLAGH
Facility: University of Minnesota Les Bolstad G.C., Falcon Heights, Minn.
Website: www.uofmgolf.com
Teaching since: 1967
Top 100 since: 1996

MIKE McGETRICK
Facility: Mike McGetrick Golf Academy, Denver, Colo.
Website: www.mcgetrickgolf.com
Teaching since: 1983
Top 100 since: 1996

BRIAN MOGG
Facility: Brian Mogg Golf Performance Center at Golden Bear G.C., Windermere, Fla.
Website: www.moggperformance.com
Teaching since: 1992
Top 100 since: 2005

BILL MORETTI
Facility: Academy of Golf at the Hills of Lakeway, Austin, Tex.
Website: www.golfdynamics.com
Teaching since: 1979
Top 100 since: 1996

JERRY MOWLDS
Facility: Pumpkin Ridge G.C., North Plains, Ore.
Website: www.pumpkinridge.com
Teaching since: 1970
Top 100 since: 1996

SCOTT MUNROE
Facility: Adios Golf Club, Coconut Creek, Fla.
Website: www.moneygolf.net
Teaching since: 1977
Top 100 since: 2009

JIM MURPHY
Facility: Jim Murphy Golf, Sugar Land, Tex.
Website: www.jimmurphygolf.com
Teaching since: 1984
Top 100 since: 2003

TOM NESS
Facility: Reunion Golf Club, Hoschton, Ga.
Website: www.chateauelanatlanta.com
Teaching since: 1972
Top 100 since: 2007

PIA NILSSON
Facility: Vision 54, Phoenix, Ariz.
Website: www.vision54.com
Teaching since: 1987
Top 100 since: 2001

DAN PASQUARIELLO
Facility: Pebble Beach Golf Academy, Pebble Beach, Calif.
Website: www.pebblebeach.com
Teaching since: 1970
Top 100 since: 2007

TOM PATRI
Facility: Friar's Head G.C., Baiting Hollow, N.Y.
Website: www.tompatri.com
Teaching since: 1981
Top 100 since: 2001

BRUCE PATTERSON
Facility: Butler National G.C., Oak Brook, Ill.
Website: None
Teaching since: 1980
Top 100 since: 2005

MIKE PERPICH
Facility: RiverPines Golf, Alpharetta, Ga.
Website: www.mikeperpich.com
Teaching since: 1976
Top 100 since: 2001

GALE PETERSON
Facility: Sea Island Golf Learning Center, St. Simons Island, Ga.
Website: www.seaisland.com
Teaching since: 1978
Top 100 since: 1996

E.J. PFISTER
Facility: Gaillardia G.C., Oklahoma City, Okla.
Website: www.ejpfistergolf.com
Teaching since: 1998
Top 100 since: 2009

DAVID PHILLIPS
Facility: Titleist Performance Institute, Oceanside, Calif.
Website: www.titleistperformanceinstitute.com
Teaching since: 1989
Top 100 since: 2001

CAROL PREISINGER
Facility: Kiawah Island Club, Johns Island, S.C.
Website: www.kiawahislandclub.com
Teaching since: 1986
Top 100 since: 2005

KIP PUTERBAUGH
Facility: Aviara Golf Academy, Carlsbad, Calif.
Website: www.aviaragolfacademy.com
Teaching since: 1972
Top 100 since: 1996

NANCY QUARCELINO
Facility: Nancy Quarcelino School of Golf, Spring Hill, Tenn.
Website: www.qsog.com
Teaching since: 1979
Top 100 since: 2003

CARL RABITO
Facility: Rabito Golf at Bolingbrook G.C., Bolingbrook, Ill.
Website: www.rabitogolf.com
Teaching since: 1987
Top 100 since: 2007

DANA RADER
Facility: Ballantyne Resort, Charlotte, N.C.
Website: www.danarader.com
Teaching since: 1980
Top 100 since: 1996

BRAD REDDING
Facility: The Resort Club at Grande Dunes, Myrtle Beach, S.C.
Website: www.grandedunes.com
Teaching since: 1984
Top 100 since: 2001

BRADY RIGGS
Facility: Woodley Lakes G.C., Van Nuys, Calif.
Website: www.bradyriggs.com
Teaching since: 1990
Top 100 since: 2007

SCOTT SACKETT
Facility: Resort Golf Schools, Scottsdale, Ariz.
Website: www.scottsackett.com
Teaching since: 1985
Top 100 since: 1999

ADAM SCHRIBER
Facility: Crystal Mountain Resort, Thompsonville, Mich.
Website: www.crystalmountain.com
Teaching since: 1984
Top 100 since: 2009

TED SHEFTIC
Facility: Ted Sheftic Learning Center, Hanover, Pa.
Website: www.tedsheftic.com
Teaching since: 1966
Top 100 since: 2003

LAIRD SMALL
Facility: Pebble Beach Golf Academy, Pebble Beach, Calif.
Website: www.pebblebeach.com
Teaching since: 1977
Top 100 since: 1996

RANDY SMITH
Facility: Royal Oaks C.C., Dallas, Tex.
Website: www.roccdallas.com
Teaching since: 1973
Top 100 since: 2001

RICK SMITH
Facility: Rick Smith Golf Academy at Tiburon, Naples, Fla.
Website: www.ricksmith.com
Teaching since: 1977
Top 100 since: 1996

TODD SONES
Facility: Impact Golf Schools at White Deer Run G.C., Vernon Hills, Ill.
Website: www.toddsones.com
Teaching since: 1982
Top 100 since: 1996

MITCHELL SPEARMAN
Facility: Manhattan Woods G.C., West Nyack, N.Y.
Website: www.mitchellspearman.com
Teaching since: 1979
Top 100 since: 1996

KELLIE STENZEL
Facility: Atlantic Golf Club, Bridgehampton, N.Y.
Website: www.kelliestenzelgolf.com
Teaching since: 1989
Top 100 since: 2009

TOM F. STICKNEY II
Facility: Bighorn Golf Club, Palm Desert, Calif.
Website: www.tomstickneygolf.com
Teaching since: 1990
Top 100 since: 2007

JON TATTERSALL
Facility: Golf Performance Partners, Atlanta, Ga.
Website: www.golfpp.com
Teaching since: 1986
Top 100 since: 2007

DR. T.J. TOMASI
Facility: PGA Learning Center, Port St. Lucie, Fla.
Website: www.tjtomasi.com
Teaching since: 1975
Top 100 since: 1999

PAUL TRITTLER
Facility: Kostis/McCord Learning Ctr., Scottsdale, Ariz.
Website: www.kostismccordlearning.com
Teaching since: 1983
Top 100 since: 1999

J.D. TURNER
Facility: The Turner Golf Group, Savannah, Ga.
Website: www.jdturnergolf.com
Teaching since: 1965
Top 100 since: 1996

STAN UTLEY
Facility: Grayhawk Learning Ctr., Scottsdale, Ariz.
Website: www.stanutleygolf.com
Teaching since: 1999
Top 100 since: 2009

CARL WELTY, JR.
Facility: Jim McLean G.S. at PGA West, La Quinta, Calif.
Website: www.jimmclean.com/usa/pga-west
Teaching since: 1965
Top 100 since: 1996

CHUCK WINSTEAD
Facility: The University Club, Baton Rouge, La.
Website: www.universityclubbr.com
Teaching since: 1993
Top 100 since: 2005

MARK WOOD
Facility: Cornerstone Club, Montrose, Colo.
Website: www.cornerstonecolorado.com
Teaching since: 1984
Top 100 since: 1999

DR. DAVID WRIGHT
Facility: Wright Balance Golf Academy, Mission Viejo, Calif.
Website: www.wrightbalance.com
Teaching since: 1982
Top 100 since: 2005

Get more information on GOLF Magazine's Top 100 Teachers and the Top Teachers by region, plus exclusive video tips and drills at www.golf.com.

EMERITUS

JIMMY BALLARD
Facility: Ballard Swing Connection, Key Largo, Fla.
Website: www.jimmyballard.com
Teaching since: 1960
Top 100 since: 1996

PEGGY KIRK BELL
Facility: Pine Needles Resort, Southern Pines, N.C.
Website: www.pineneedles-midpines.com
Teaching since: 1958
Top 100 since: 1996

CHUCK COOK
Facility: Chuck Cook Golf Academy at Barton Creek C.C., Austin, Tex.
Website: www.bartoncreek.com
Teaching since: 1975
Top 100 since: 1996

MANUEL DE LA TORRE
Facility: Milwaukee C.C., River Hills, Wis.
Website: www.manueldelatorregolf.com
Teaching since: 1948
Top 100 since: 1996

JIM FLICK
Facility: TaylorMade Performance and Research Lab, Carlsbad, Calif.
Website: www.jimflick.com
Teaching since: 1954
Top 100 since: 1996

MICHAEL HEBRON
Facility: Smithtown Landing G.C., Smithtown, N.Y.
Website: www.mikehebron.com
Teaching since: 1967
Top 100 since: 1996

DAVID LEADBETTER
Facility: David Leadbetter Golf Academy, Champions Gate, Fla.
Website: www.davidleadbetter.com
Teaching since: 1976
Top 100 since: 1996

JIM McLEAN
Facility: Jim McLean Golf Schools at Doral Resort, Miami, Fla.
Website: www.jimmclean.com
Teaching since: 1975
Top 100 since: 1996

EDDIE MERRINS
Facility: Bel-Air C.C., Los Angeles, Calif.
Website: www.eddiemerrins.com
Teaching since: 1957
Top 100 since: 1996

DAVE PELZ
Facility: Pelz Golf, Austin, Tex.
Website: www.pelzgolf.com
Teaching since: 1976
Top 100 since: 1996

PHIL RITSON
Facility: Phil Ritson Golf Your Way, Winter Garden, Fla.
Website: www.ocngolf.com
Teaching since: 1950
Top 100 since: 1996

PHIL RODGERS
Facility: Carlton Oaks C.C., San Diego, Calif.
Website: None
Teaching since: 1977
Top 100 since: 1996

CRAIG SHANKLAND
Facility: Craig Shankland G.S., Daytona Beach, Fla.
Website: None
Teaching since: 1957
Top 100 since: 1996

DR. JIM SUTTIE
Facility: Suttie Academies at TwinEagles, Naples, Fla.
Website: www.jimsuttie.com
Teaching since: 1972
Top 100 since: 1996

BOB TOSKI
Facility: Toski-Battersby Golf Learning Ctr., Coconut Creek, Fla.
Website: www.learn-golf.com
Teaching since: 1956
Top 100 since: 1996

DR. GARY WIREN
Facility: Trump Int., W. Palm Beach, Fla.
Website: www.garywiren.com
Teaching since: 1955
Top 100 since: 1996

EDITOR
David M. Clarke

CREATIVE DIRECTOR
Paul Crawford

EXECUTIVE EDITOR
Eamon Lynch

ART DIRECTOR
Paul Ewen

MANAGING EDITORS
David DeNunzio (Instruction), Gary Perkinson
(Production), Robert Sauerhaft (Equipment)

EDITOR AT LARGE
Connell Barrett

DEPUTY MANAGING EDITOR
Michael Chwasky (Instruction & Equipment)

SENIOR EDITORS
Alan Bastable, Joseph Passov (Travel/Course
Rankings), Michael Walker Jr.

DEPUTY ART DIRECTOR
Karen Ha

PHOTO EDITORS
Carrie Boretz (Associate), Jesse Reiter (Assistant)

SENIOR WRITER
Cameron Morfit

ASSISTANT EDITOR
Steven Beslow

ADMINISTRATIVE ASSISTANT
Jessica Marksbury

PUBLISHER
Dick Raskopf

ASSOCIATE ADVERTISING DIRECTOR
Nathan Stamos

DIRECTOR OF BUSINESS DEVELOPMENT
Brad J. Felenstein

GENERAL MANAGER
Peter Greer

VP & GENERAL MANAGER (GOLF.COM)
Ken Fuchs

BUSINESS DEVELOPEMENT MANAGER
Russ Vance

EXECUTIVE DIRECTOR, MARKETING
Bruce Revman

HUMAN RESOURCES DIRECTOR
Liz Mattila

EDITOR, SPORT ILLUSTRATED GROUP
Terry McDonell

EXECUTIVE EDITOR
Michael Bevans

MANAGING EDITOR, SI.COM
Paul Fichtenbaum

**ASST. MANAGING EDITOR,
GOLF PLUS/GOLF.COM**
James P. Herre

V.P., ADVERTISING SALES
Jeff Griffing

CHIEF MARKETING OFFICER
Andrew R. Judelson

PRESIDENT, SI DIGITAL
Jeff Price

V.P., CONSUMER MARKETING
John Reese

V.P., COMMUNICATIONS
Scott Novak

NEWS GROUP

EXECUTIVE V.P.
John Squires

PRESIDENT & GROUP PUBLISHER
Mark Ford

SENIOR V.P. & GROUP GENERAL MGR.
John B. Reuter

GOLF.com

EXECUTIVE EDITOR
Charlie Hanger

EXECUTIVE PRODUCER
Christopher Shade

DEPUTY EDITOR
David Dusek

PRODUCERS
Ryan Reiterman, Anne Szeker

ASSOCIATE ART DIRECTOR
Omar Sharif

SR. AD OPERATIONS MANAGER
Elise LeScoezec

PUBLISHER
Richard Fraiman

GENERAL MANAGER
Steven Sandonato

**EXECUTIVE DIRECTOR,
MARKETING SERVICES**
Carol Pittard

DIRECTOR, RETAIL & SPECIAL SALES
Tom Mifsud

DIRECTOR, NEW PRODUCT DEVELOPMENT
Peter Harper

**ASSISTANT DIRECTOR,
BOOKAZINE MARKETING**
Laura Adam

**ASSISTANT PUBLISHING DIRECTOR,
BRAND MARKETING**
Joy Butts

ASSOCIATE COUNSEL
Helen Wan

BRAND & LICENSING MANAGER
Alexandra Bliss

DESIGN & PREPRESS MANAGER
Anne-Michelle Gallero

BOOK PRODUCTION MANAGER
Susan Chodakiewicz

THANK YOU!
Glenn Buonocore, Jim Childs, Caroline DeNunzio,
Lauren Hall, Jennifer Jacobs, Suzanne Janso,
Brynn Joyce, Robert Marasco, Amy Migliaccio,
Brooke Reger, D.J. Infante "Pop-Pop" Sweetum Deez,
Ilene Schrieder, Adrianna Tierno, Alex Voznesenskiy,
Sydney Webber

THE BEST
SHORT GAME
INSTRUCTION
BOOK EVER!

WORDS

GOLF MAGAZINE'S
TOP 100 TEACHERS IN AMERICA
with
DAVID DeNUNZIO

BOOK DESIGN

PAUL EWEN

BOOK & COVER PHOTOGRAPHY

ANGUS MURRAY

SI IMAGING

GEOFFREY A. MICHAUD (Director)
DAN LARKIN, ROBERT M. THOMPSON

ADDITIONAL PHOTOGRAPHY

BOB ATKINS 30-35

JOHN BIEVER/SI 118-119

ROBERT BECK/SI 90-91, 150-151

D2 PRODUCTIONS 47, 102-103, 121, 156

JAMES DRAKE/SI 16-17

GETTY IMAGES 23

JOHN IACONO/SI 14-15

RICHARD MACKSON/SI 12-13

SCHECTER LEE 20-22, 28, 29, 164-167

JESSE REITER 46-47

MARC SEROTA 157

ROB TRINGALI 176, 184-187

ILLUSTRATIONS

ROBIN GRIGGS (1957-2008) 38-45

MIRTOART.COM 69, 85, 117

BARRY ROSS 67, 83, 113, 143

CHARTS & GRAPHICS

KAREN HA